GW01236822

# TECHNIQUES IN Cake Design

# TECHNIQUES IN Cake Design

⋮

### Geraldine RANDLESOME

## ACKNOWLEDGEMENTS

Geraldine Randlesome would like to thank Lily Con, Bill, and Gadi Hoz for their work, and Joan Davidson for the little "extras". Finally, to the cake decorating teachers and students both living and deceased who stimulated my interest in this art form. Therefore this book is dedicated to the many people who saw the first "Floating Collar" and continually requested a "How To" book.

PUBLISHED 1986 by Geraldine Randlesome
3 Tannery Court, Richmond Hill, Ontario L4C 5S4   CANADA

Copyright.

ISBN 0-9692523-0-7

All rights reserved. No part of this publication may be reproduced, stored in a retrieval system, or transmitted in any form or by any means, electronic, mechanical, photocopying, recording, or otherwise, without the prior written permission of the author.

Design and Production by Fortunato Aglialoro & Linda Pellowe/
FALCOM DESIGN & COMMUNICATIONS

Photographed by Vassilios (Bill) Krespis and Gadi Hoz.

Line Illustrations by Lily Con

Typesetting by ATTIC TYPESETTING, Inc.

Colour Separations by LASERSHARP INC., TORONTO
Printed and Bound in Hong Kong by SCANNER ART SERVICES INC., TORONTO.

*This book is dedicated to my husband Alan for all his wonderful support, and to my two children, Paul and Nicole. Thank you Nikki for making the Blue Sparkle Cake. And finally, to my parents who have helped me so much with the little "extras".*

# Contents

| | |
|---|---|
| INTRODUCTION | 7 |
| RECIPES FOR CAKES | 8 |
| RECIPES FOR ICING | 9 |
| COVERING A CAKE BOARD | 10 |
| COVERING A CAKE | 11 |
| DOWELLING A CAKE | 14 |
| EMBOSSED CARDS | 15 |
| FILET CROCHET | 15 |
| FLOOD-WORK | 16 |
| MOLD MAKING | 16 |

## Beginners

| | |
|---|---|
| Pink Baby Cake | 21 |
| Blue Birthday Cake with Sparkles | 23 |
| Yellow Cake with Cameo | 24 |
| Yellow Cake with Basket | 25 |
| Yellow Cake with Embroidery | 26 |
| Yellow Cake with Daisies | 27 |
| Three-Tier Art Decor | 28 |

## Intermediate

| | |
|---|---|
| Two-Tier Ruffle Cake | 29 |
| Two-Tier Beige Cake | 30 |
| Blue One-Tier Cake | 32 |

## Advanced

| | |
|---|---|
| Two-Tier Yellow Cake | 34 |
| Two-Tier Oval Cake | 36 |
| Blue Cake—Double String Work | 42 |

## New Techniques

| | |
|---|---|
| Anniversary Cake | 44 |
| Anniversary Music Box | 47 |
| Dutch Iris | 47 |
| Cross-Over Cake | 50 |
| Hibiscus | 51 |
| Cymbidium Cake | 53 |
| No Bridge String Work Cake | 56 |
| Two-Tier White Cake | 62 |
| White & Burgundy Cake | 64 |

## Floating Collars

| | |
|---|---|
| Beige Double Collar Cake 1983 | 66 |
| Winning Cake from London | 78 |
| Green & White Cake | 80 |
| Two-Tier White Floating Collar Cake | 84 |
| Two-Tier Pink Cake with Roses | 90 |
| Beige Cake with Upside-down String Work | 92 |
| Double Floating Collar Cake | 94 |

## Patterns

| | |
|---|---|
| Lace | 97 |
| Embroidery | 98 |

# Introduction

My experience of cake decorating and teaching has shown me that if the basics or details of the art of cake decorating are taught properly, the student will be encouraged to: go on and develop their own style; be creative and original in their thinking; bring new ideas that will enhance the art; and give many years of satisfaction and pleasure to both the cake designer and the client.

I remember with great satisfaction when my first floating collar cake was put on display in Kentucky in 1983. Hundreds of admirers and cake decorators spent countless hours, looking at the work trying to see if the collars were held up by clear plastic or glass, as the cake had travelled over 500 miles by road and arrived without damage. The same was true when I took a floating collar cake to South Africa in 1984 via London, England. The South Africans who took my class on the floating collar, ended the lesson having achieved this 'impossible' task of creating the floating collar, and I *still* get photos showing how they have enhanced the collar with their own skills and ideas.

This book was written in response to the many requests from both novices and experienced cake decorators who are looking for more challenging ideas and the encouragement to try something new.

The intent of the book is to create an easy-to-follow, complete step-by-step guide to the covering and decorating of cakes using fondant icing. Starting with the beginner, graduating to the intermediate, then advanced and finally, posing new techniques to challenge.

Many of the gum paste flowers shown are detailed in my previous book and therefore not repeated here. If this book challenges you and helps you to have confidence to try something new, then the effort and work has all been worthwhile.

I wish the reader many years of satisfying cake decorating.

*Geraldine*

# Recipes for Cakes

Many people have their own favourite recipes for cakes, so I am only going to include two recipes which I have found to be very suitable for fondant icing.

**Fruit Cake**

Recipe for a 20.3 cm (8") round cake

INGREDIENTS

*Mixed dried fruit i.e. raisins, sultanas and or dates. 1.2k (2½ lbs)*

*Nuts Pecans or Almonds 200 g (6 ozs)*

*Mixed peel 125 g (4 ozs)*

*Glace cherries 200 g (6 ozs)*

*Sweet butter 300 g (10 ozs)*

*Brown sugar 300 g (10 ozs)*

*Eggs (large) 7 (7)*

*All purpose flour (Self-raising flour) 350 g (12 ozs)*

*Salt ¼ level teasp (¼ level teasp)*

*Mixed spices 10 ml (2 level teasp)*

*Brandy (optional) 45 ml (3 tablesp)*

*Orange (both juice and rind) 1 (1)*

*Lemon (both juice and rind) 1 (1)*

**Method**

Wash all the fruit and cherries and let dry for 2 days. Line the cake tin with several layers of brown paper, with the final layer being either a wax paper or a greaseproof paper.

Cream the butter and sugar together very well. Beat in the eggs one at a time.
Sieve the dry ingredients together and mix one cup of the dry ingredients into the fruit, nuts and grated rind mixture.
Add gradually to the creamed mixture, with a little of the lemon and orange juices. Finally mix the brandy into the mixture.
Pour the mixture into the prepared cake tin and smooth the top of the cake with dampened fingers.

Bake in a slow oven 275 deg (140 deg C) for approximately 4–5 hours.

When cold remove from the tin and re-wrap until the cake is required.

**Almond Cake**

30.5 cm (12") round cake

INGREDIENTS

*Cooking almond paste (marzipan) 1 kg (2 lbs)*

*White sugar 500 g (1 lb)*

*Eggs (large) 12 (12)*

*Cake & Pastry Flour (All-purpose flour) 250 g (8 ozs)*

*Apricot brandy (optional) 45 ml (3 tablesp)*

Prepare the cake tin as for the fruit cake

**Method**

Cut the almond paste into small pieces and place into a mixer, add brandy and sugar and beat very well together.
Gradually add the eggs and beat at low speed for 10–15 mins until very smooth. Finally fold in the flour very gently.
Pour the mixture into the tin and bake 350 deg (175 deg.C) for approximately 2–2½ hours.

This cake will keep fresh up to a week, and can be served with fresh fruit, fresh whipping cream, or ice cream.

# Recipes for Icing

## Royal Icing

Many people feel that I have a secret for my string work. I have found that the best royal icing to use is from egg whites, not meringue powder. Meringue powder royal icing does not have the strength or the stretch as egg white royal icing.

INGREDIENTS

*1 glass bowl.*

*1 medium egg white.*

*8-10 ozs (225g-300g) sifted icing sugar.*

*1/8 teasp gum arabic. (for strength)*

*1/4 teasp liquid glucose. (for stretch)*

Place the egg white into the glass bowl. Slowly add the sifted icing sugar (teasp by teasp) while mixing the icing with a knife. Continue mixing until the icing is a soft peak, then add the sifted gum arabic, mix well. Continue beating until a stiff peak is reached then add the glucose mix well.

Take the knife out of the bowl, cover the bowl with plastic wrap, then a damp cloth. This icing will keep up to three days for string work, although it must be freshly stirred each morning. You may also have to add a small amount of extra sifted icing sugar.

## Fondant (Plastic or Sugar Paste) Icing

INGREDIENTS

*Gelatin 15 ml (1 pkt)*

*Cold water 60 ml (1/4 cup)*

Mix the above together, let stand 5 mins then melt the mixture over a saucepan of hot water over a gentle heat until completely dissolved. *(Do Not Overheat).*

*Icing Sugar 900 g (2 lbs)*

Sift the icing sugar into a bowl, making a well in the center of the icing sugar.

*Glucose 1/2 cup (1/2 cup)*

*Glycerine (optional) 15 ml (1 tablesp)*

Add the above ingredients to the heated gelatin, stirring well until a smooth mixture. Pour the mixture into the icing sugar.
With a spoon stir the icing sugar from the sides of the bowl into the mixture.
When stiff turn the mixture onto the counter and knead in the remainder of the sugar. Wrap in a plastic wrap, and let rest for 2 hours before using.

## Pastillage

There are many different recipes for pastillage. The one I used for the music box (50 Anniversary Cake) is a very simple recipe.
Sift one teasp of gum arabic into a cup of royal icing. Work in extra sifted icing sugar until pliable. Wrap well in plastic wrap until ready to use. When drying any pieces of pastillage it is always best to keep turning the pieces over to allow for even drying.

## Covering a Cake Board

*Step 1:* Brush the cake board with clear piping gel. See figure 1.

*Step 2:* Place the board on a small container to elevate. See figure 2.

*Step 3:* Dust the counter top with a small amount of cornstarch and roll out the fondant. See figure 3. When large enough to cover the board, gently lift the fondant on to the board and roll the rolling pin over the fondant to release the air. See figure 4.

*Step 4:* Trim the excess fondant from the side of the board. See figure 5.

*Step 5:* Set aside and always let dry overnight before placing the cake on the board.

Fig. 1

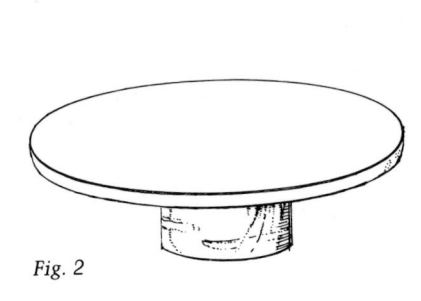

Fig. 2

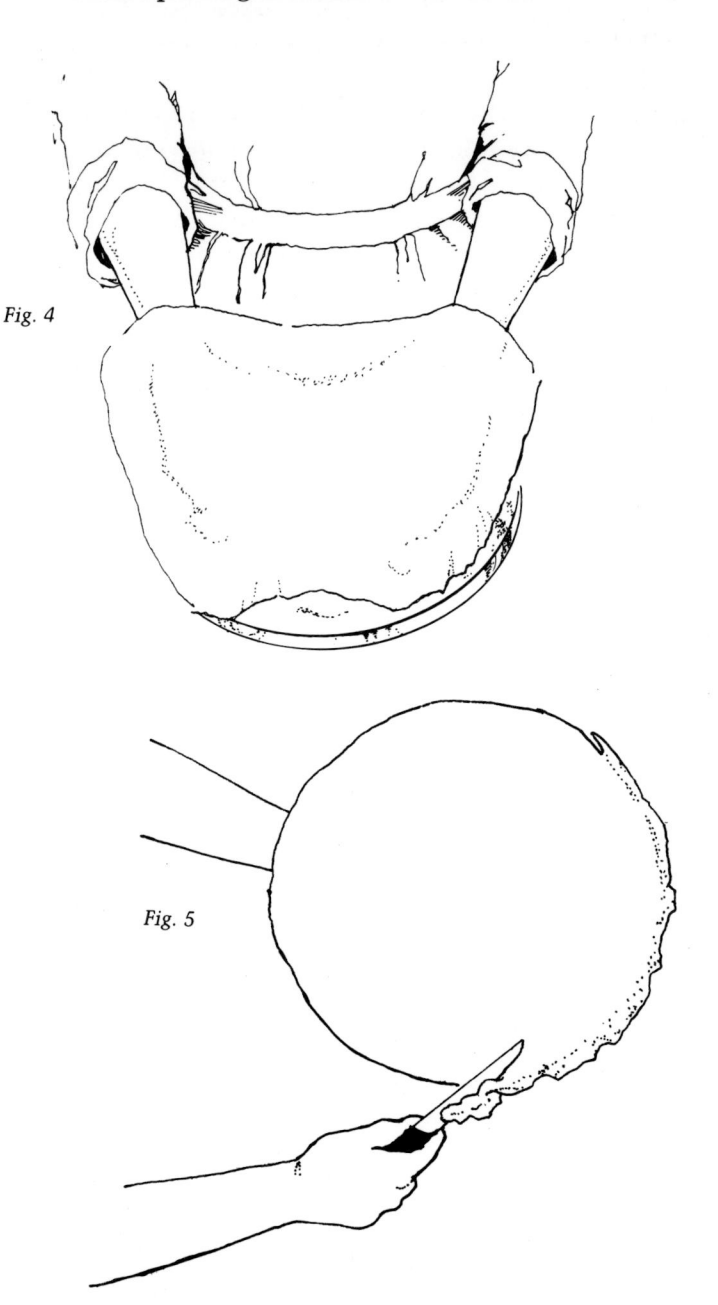

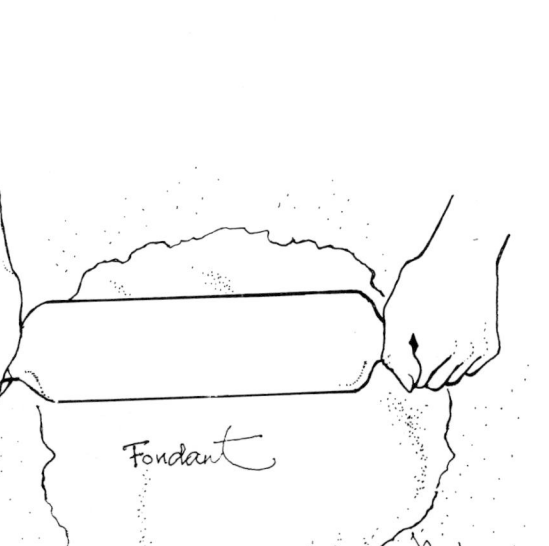

Fig. 3

Fig. 4

Fig. 5

# Covering a Cake

It is always much easier to cover a cake if the cake is elevated on a stand with a smaller radius than the cake.

If you are covering a styrofoam dummy first, sand the top edges of the form to create a softer look. Brush the dummy cake with piping gel (or boiled and sifted apricot jam, or vodka) if you are using a real cake. *See figure 1*. Set aside on the dummy.

*Fig. 1*

For rolling out the fondant, use either a lightly oiled large plastic sheet, or first dust the counter with a small amount of cornstarch. Lightly oil the rolling pin. When the fondant has been rolled out large enough to cover the cake, gently slide both hands underneath the fondant and gently place it on the cake. Roll the top of the cake with the rolling pin to release any air, and with the sides of your hands, gently lift and smooth the sides. *See figure 2*. Trim the bottom edge of the cake by placing a knife against the bottom of the cake to trim off the excess fondant. *See figure 3*. Gently lift and place the cake in the centre of the board. If crimper work is required, it must be done immediately before the fondant dries.

*Fig. 2*

To mark the cake with a pattern, using adding machine tape 1¼" wide (3.5 cm) to make a false collar. Tape the two edges together, *see figure 4*, and gently slide the collar off the cake. Keep

*Fig. 3*

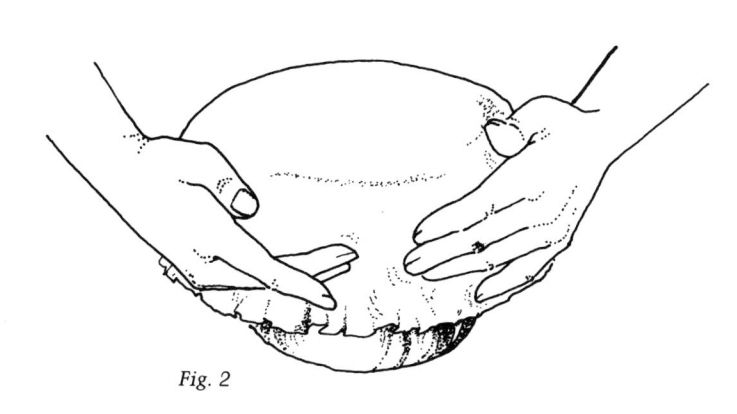

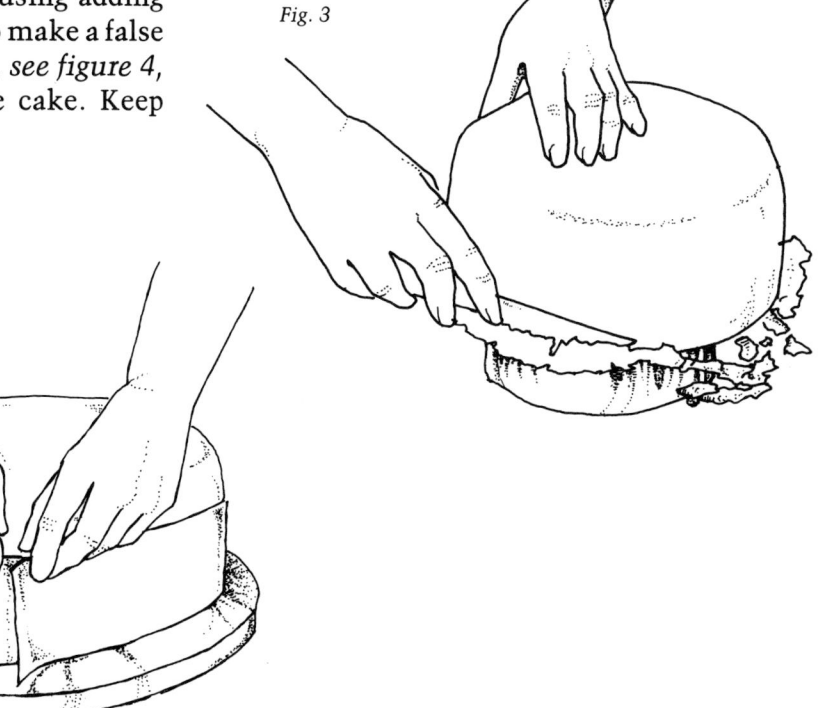

*Fig. 4*

# 12 Covering a Cake

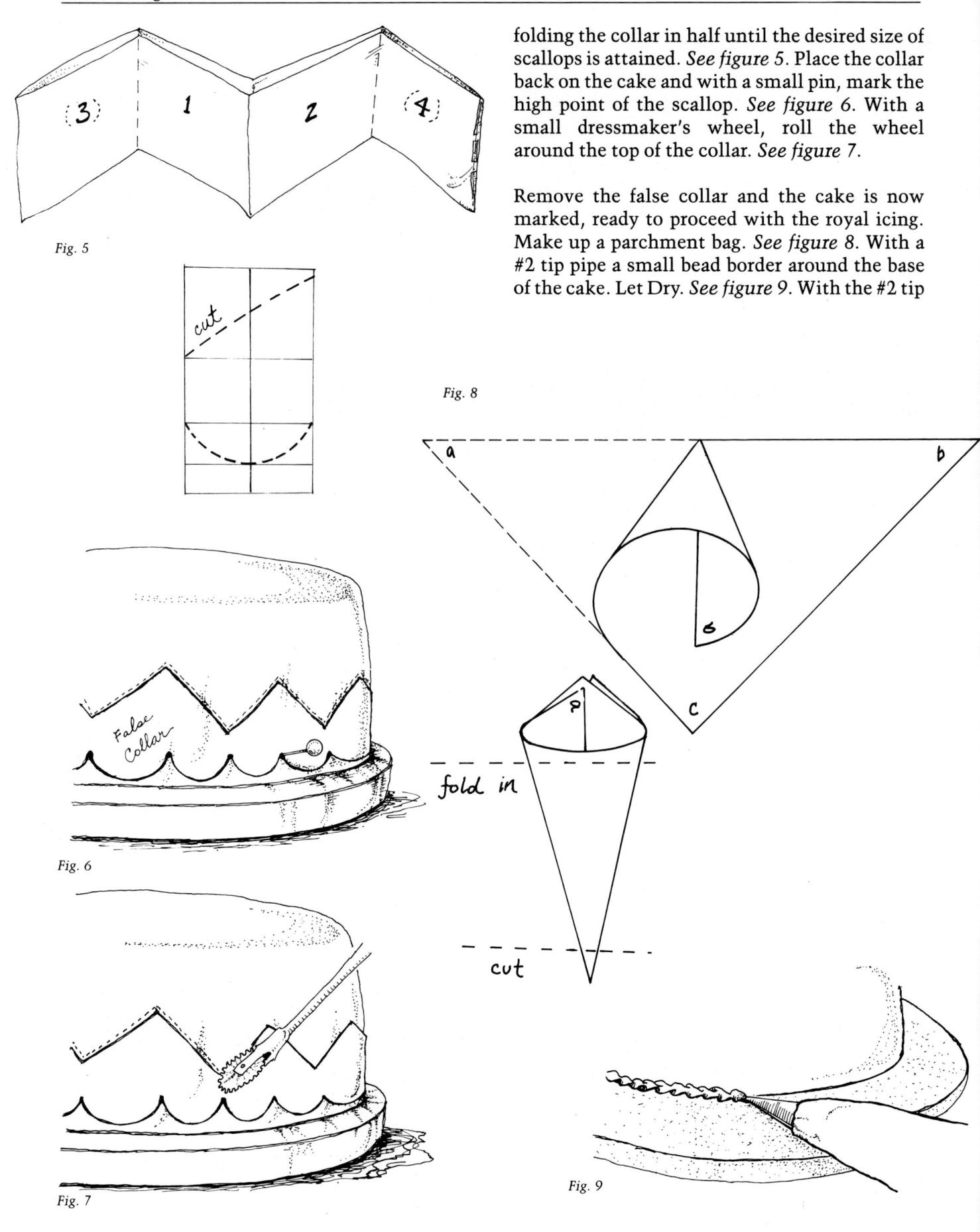

*Fig. 5*

folding the collar in half until the desired size of scallops is attained. *See figure 5*. Place the collar back on the cake and with a small pin, mark the high point of the scallop. *See figure 6*. With a small dressmaker's wheel, roll the wheel around the top of the collar. *See figure 7*.

Remove the false collar and the cake is now marked, ready to proceed with the royal icing. Make up a parchment bag. *See figure 8*. With a #2 tip pipe a small bead border around the base of the cake. Let Dry. *See figure 9*. With the #2 tip

*Fig. 6*

*Fig. 7*

*Fig. 8*

*Fig. 9*

pipe a line of scallops all around the cake. *See figure 10*. The second row should start approximately 1/4" (7mm) in from the first scallop and ending within 1/4" (7mm) from the end. Repeat for the 3rd, 4th, and 5th rows starting and ending within the shorter distance. See figure 11. Let dry. The 6th row must be piped all away around the length of the first scallop. (This solid line will help strengthen the bridge). Let dry. Mix up flood-in icing to the count of 10, (you can add colour if required) and flood-in the bridge work. (This will add both colour and strength to the bridge). With a 0 tip pipe strings from the top marked line down to the bridge. Let dry. *See figure 12*. With a 0 tip pipe the lace pieces onto a small sheet of wax paper. Let dry. *See figure 13*. To attach the lace pieces to the cake, pipe 4 small dots onto the top of the strings, and very gently attach the lace pieces to the dots. (Always attach the lace pieces at a slight angle, it creates a much softer look). *See figure 14*. To finish your cake, cover the side of the cake with a ribbon, attaching the ribbon with a small pin. *See figure 15*.

Fig. 10

Fig. 11

Fig. 12

Fig. 13

Fig. 14

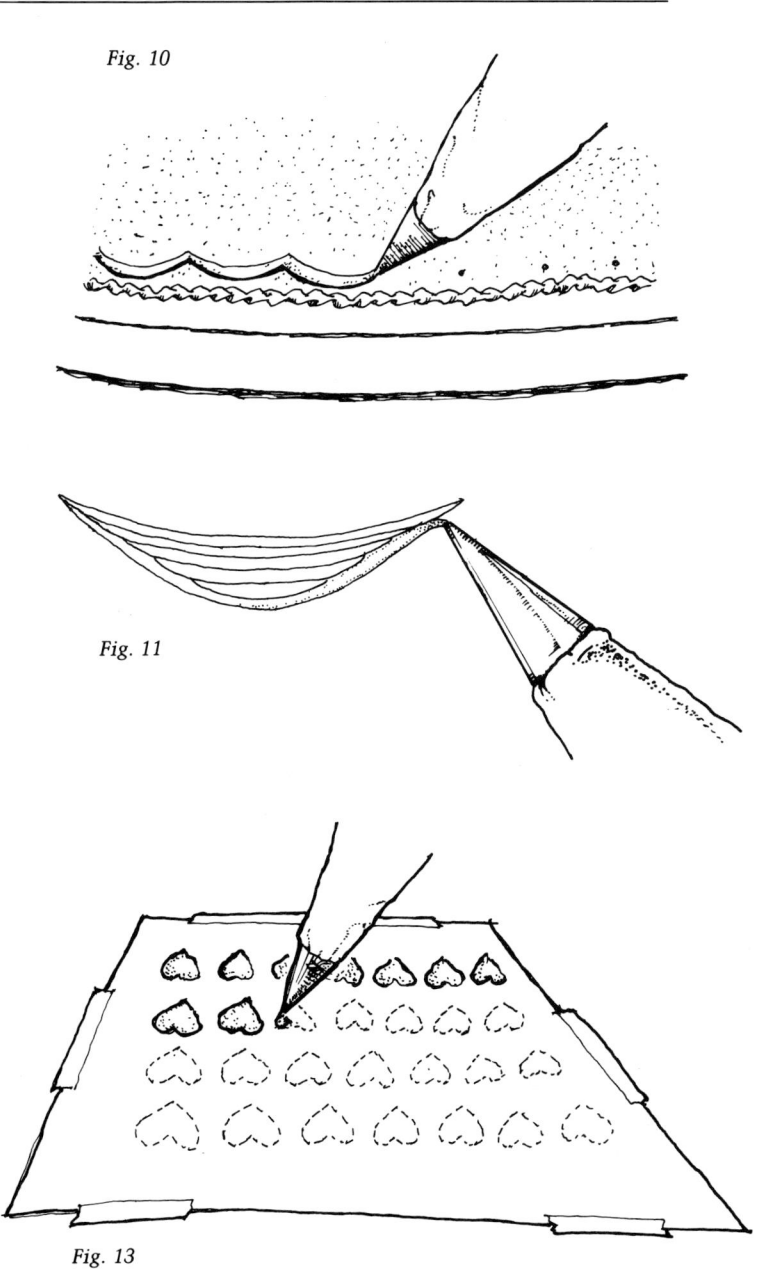

Fig. 15

# Dowelling a Cake

*Fig. 1*

All tiered cakes should be dowelled to prevent any accidents. Soft cakes in the warm weather can slip, or sink into the cake they are sitting on. Most dowels are made from ¼" (7 mm) wood, or for heavy liquor type cakes, a ½" (13 mm) dowel may be required.

First with a template, mark the top of the cakes where you are going to place the pillars. *See figure 1*. Remove the template and with a meat skewer or long needle, push the needle into and down to the base of the cake. Remove the needle and replace it with the wooden dowel. *See figure 2*. Many Australian style cakes are better supported when the dowels go into the cake and through the hollow pillar, *see figure 3*, although the towel can be cut off at the top of the cake. Attach the pillars with royal icing and set the top tier on the pillars.

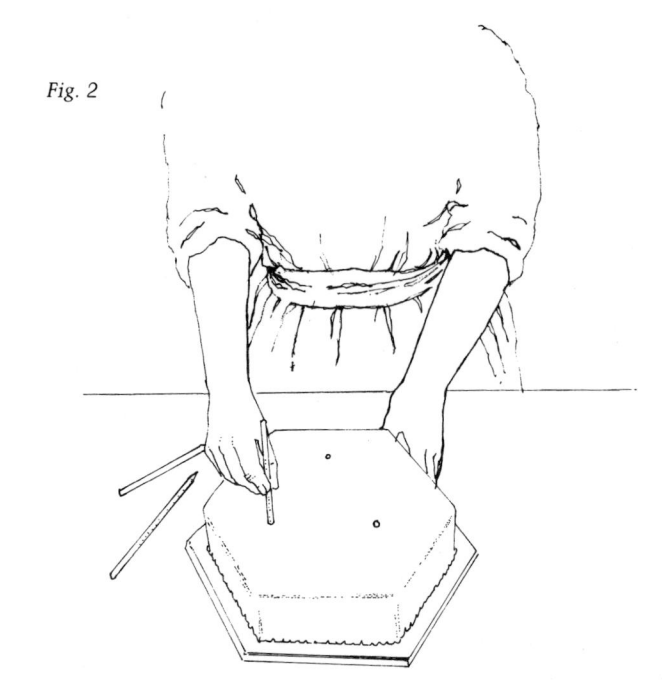

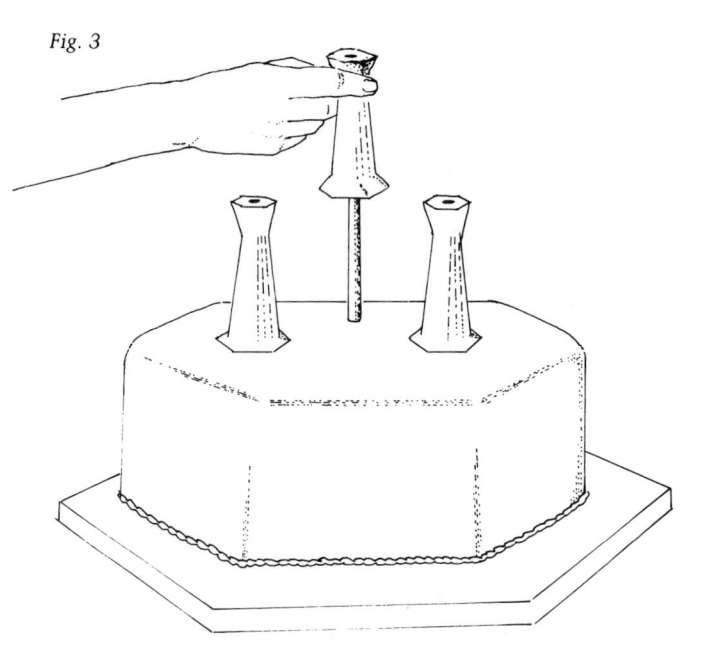

*Fig. 2*

*Fig. 3*

# Embossed Cards

The purpose of embossed cards is to allow a design to be transferred to a soft fondant cake. Cut a small piece of soft cardboard to the desired height of the cake. Outline your pattern on a sheet of tracing paper. Reverse the sheet of tracing paper and outline over the pattern. Place the sheet of tracing paper onto the cardboard, then outline the pattern. *See figure 1.* Remove the tracing paper, and with a #1 or #2 tip and royal icing pipe the outline. Let Dry. *See figure 2.* These cards can only be pressed into freshly covered fondant cakes. The cards can also be stored for future use.

*Fig. 1*

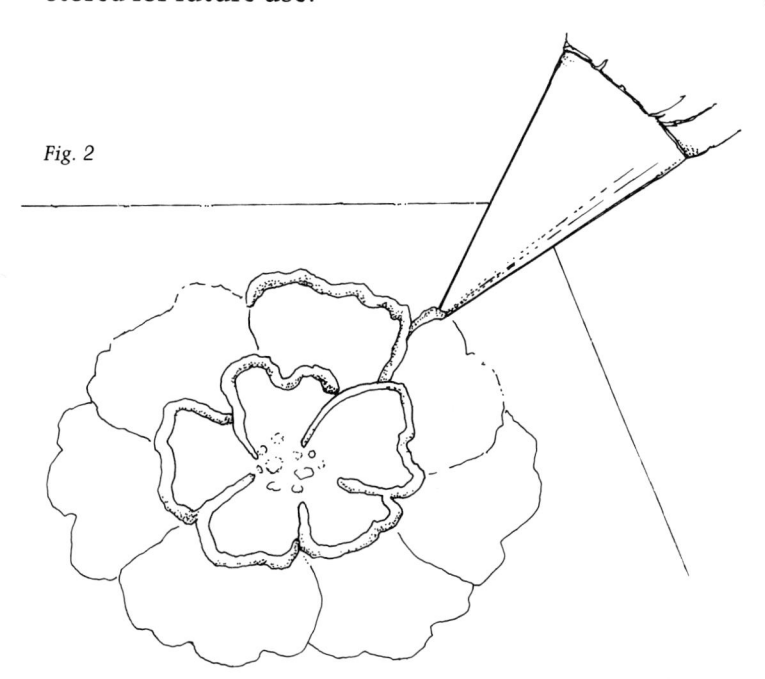

*Fig. 2*

# Filet Crochet

I would like to thank Betty L. Van Norstrand of Poughkeepsie, N.Y. for allowing me to include the beautiful technique she designed and taught in her class "Needlework in Icing".

The filet crochet technique looks very beautiful made up on birthday cards, small cameos and cakes.

Purchase some filet crochet pattern books for size of pattern etc. Make a plaque from either gum paste or fondant, and while still soft roll a specialized rolling pin gently over the plaque to create the effect of a canvas. (The rolling pin can be purchased from specialized cake decorating stores). Let dry. Starting from the center of the plaque and following the numbers of squares, count out the pattern frame. With a #1 tip and starting at the top of the pattern, pipe a small dot of icing into the square. (Do not pipe more than 6–8 dots at any one time). Working with a large hat pin and a small piece of damp sponge, run the hat pin across the damp sponge, then cut the dot through the center to create a small upside down "V". Continue counting the squares, piping and cutting through the dots until all the pattern has been completed.

Let dry, then attach to the cake with royal icing.

# Flood-work

Colour flow is also known as flow in, run sugar or flood-in.

Before starting any type of run in work, it is always best to make the icing up the day before using to help eliminate any air bubbles in the mixture. Always mix the pre-made icing in a glass bowl, stirring slowly with a knife as you add a small amount of water until the desired count is reached. (Count means that when you cut through the icing with the flat side of the knife, and slowly count to 10, the icing should be joined back together, showing no marks or impression).

Draw your pattern on a sheet of tracing paper, and place the paper on a plexiglass (or glass) square. Cover the paper with either cooking film or thin plastic wrap and tape it down. Outline the pattern with a #1 or #2 tip, and then with the run in icing, flood the pattern outlined. When working on collars, you must rotate the work so that you are working on both sides at once. Do not start at one side and work around to the other side, as the first section of your work will start to dry and a line will show, as you cannot blend dry run in with wet run in. Tap the work lightly on the table and place in the oven at 200° for 15 minutes, leaving the oven door open and the oven turned off. This allows the work to crust over. Leave the run in work for approximately 48 hours before using.

# Mold Making

There are many ways to make molds. Chocolate, plaster of paris (which can be very expensive to purchase) or modelling clay are three suggestions.

Knead the required amount of Modelling clay very well. Take the object you wish to have a mold for (leaves, flowers, a cameo) and with a brush, dust the object with cornstarch and press the object into the clay. Remove the object making sure that you can see a very clear reverse impression. Bake the object on a wooden bread board in the oven at 275° (140 deg. C) for 15-25 minutes depending on the size of the mold. Let the object cool and it is ready for use.

All the molded pieces shown in this book are made from gum paste that has had a large amount of cornstarch added to make the gum paste very tight. Dust the gum paste lightly and press into the mold. Pull the paste out of the mold and check to see the quality of the details. Cut around the shape and place on to the cake with royal icing. If the molds become too sticky, wash the molds with warm water taking care to dry, and dust lightly with cornstarch before using again.

THREE-TIER ART DECOR

PINK BABY CAKE

YELLOW CAKE WITH DAISIES

YELLOW CAKES

YELLOW CAKE WITH EMBROIDERY

YELLOW CAKE WITH BASKET

BLUE BIRTHDAY CAKE WITH SPARKLES

# Beginners

## Pink Baby Cake

This is a very simple style of cake for a beginner. It covers crimper work, ribbon insertion and a very simple gum paste bib.

*Step 1:* To make the bib, roll out gum paste thinly and cut out two bibs with a cutter. On one of the bibs, cut the top section off. *See figure 1.* Lay the bibs on a lightly coated cornstarch surface and ruffle the bibs as in figure 2. Lightly coat the lower bib with gum glue and attach both bibs together. *See figure 3.* Set aside until dry. Once dry, dust the edge with dusting powder.

Fig. 1

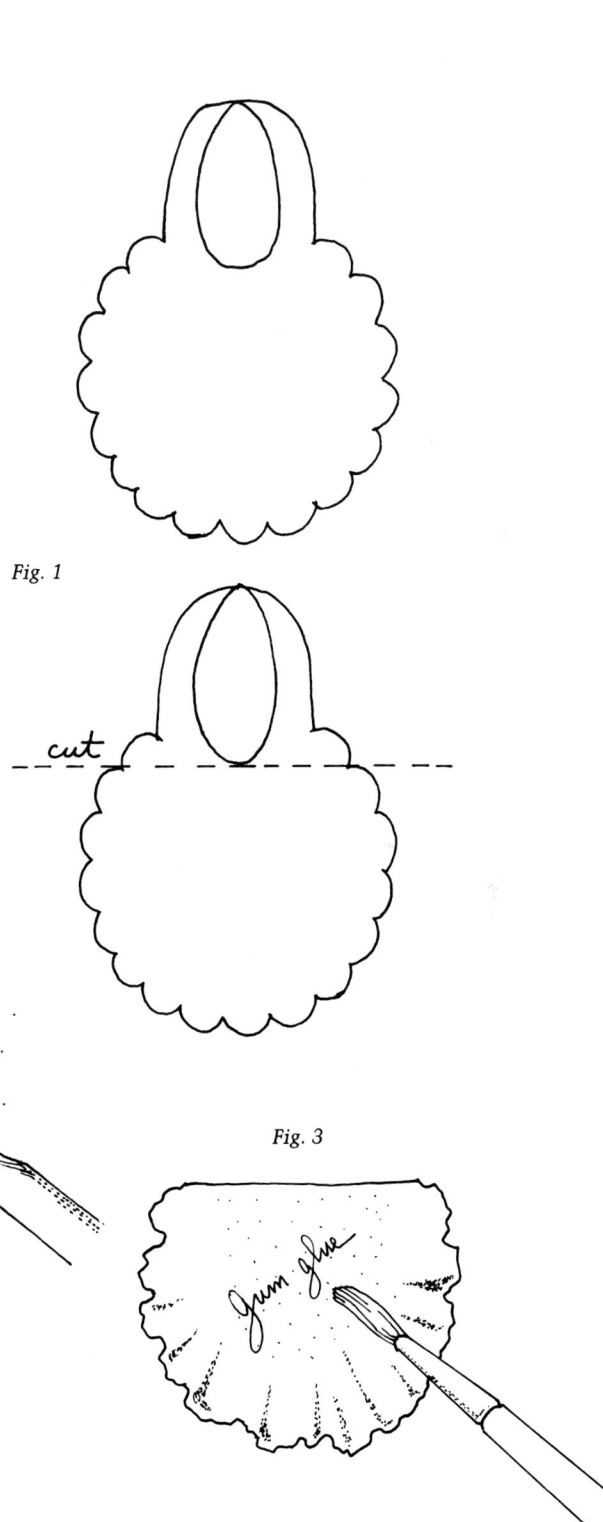

Fig. 2

Fig. 3

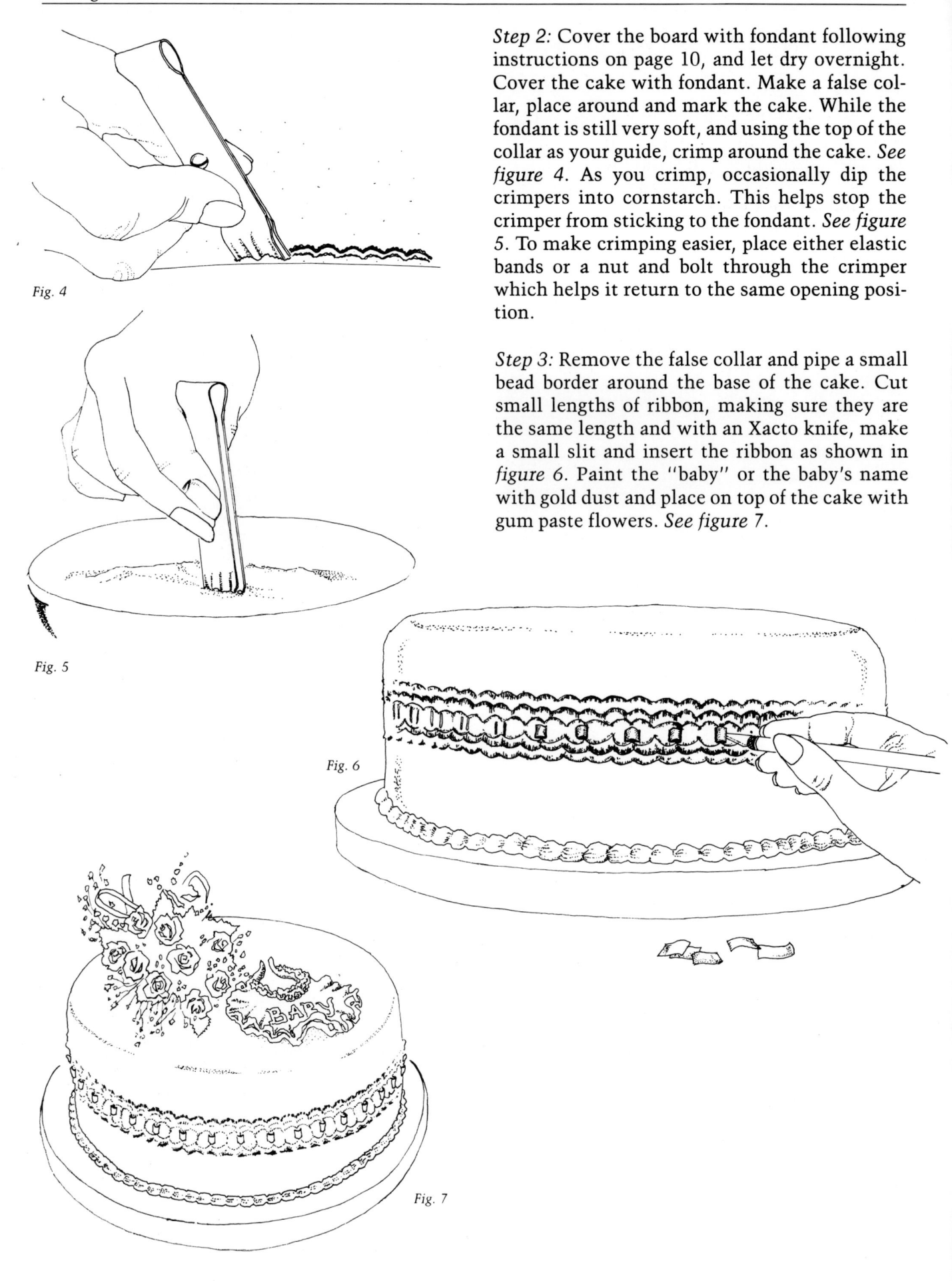

*Fig. 4*

*Fig. 5*

*Fig. 6*

*Fig. 7*

*Step 2:* Cover the board with fondant following instructions on page 10, and let dry overnight. Cover the cake with fondant. Make a false collar, place around and mark the cake. While the fondant is still very soft, and using the top of the collar as your guide, crimp around the cake. *See figure 4.* As you crimp, occasionally dip the crimpers into cornstarch. This helps stop the crimper from sticking to the fondant. *See figure 5.* To make crimping easier, place either elastic bands or a nut and bolt through the crimper which helps it return to the same opening position.

*Step 3:* Remove the false collar and pipe a small bead border around the base of the cake. Cut small lengths of ribbon, making sure they are the same length and with an Xacto knife, make a small slit and insert the ribbon as shown in *figure 6*. Paint the "baby" or the baby's name with gold dust and place on top of the cake with gum paste flowers. *See figure 7.*

# Blue Birthday Cake with Sparkles

*Step 1:* Bake a chocolate, lemon or white birthday cake and cool overnight. Cover the cake with fondant following instructions on page 11. Pipe a small star border around the base of the cake and let dry 1 hour.

*Step 2:* Polish the chocolate molds with a soft, dry cloth. (This will help release the chocolates when set and gives them more shine). In a glass bowl, melt the chocolate compound over a pot of hot water, covering the bowl with a paper towel so that no steam drips into the chocolate. *See figure 1.* (You may also melt the chocolate in a microwave oven at the defrost level for 5 minutes, or in a conventional oven at 200° for approximately 5 minutes). When the chocolate has melted, stir the chocolate and spoon into molds. *See figure 2.* Gently tap the molds to release any air bubbles and place in the freezer for 2 minutes. Remove the molds from the freezer and gently tap them on the counter to loosen the chocolates and carefully tip them out.

*Step 3:* Prepare a small parchment bag with a #2 tip. Add a small amount of melted chocolate into the paper bag and pipe the back of the chocolates and place them at random on the cake. *See figure 3.* Place the appropriate number of sparkles on the cake.

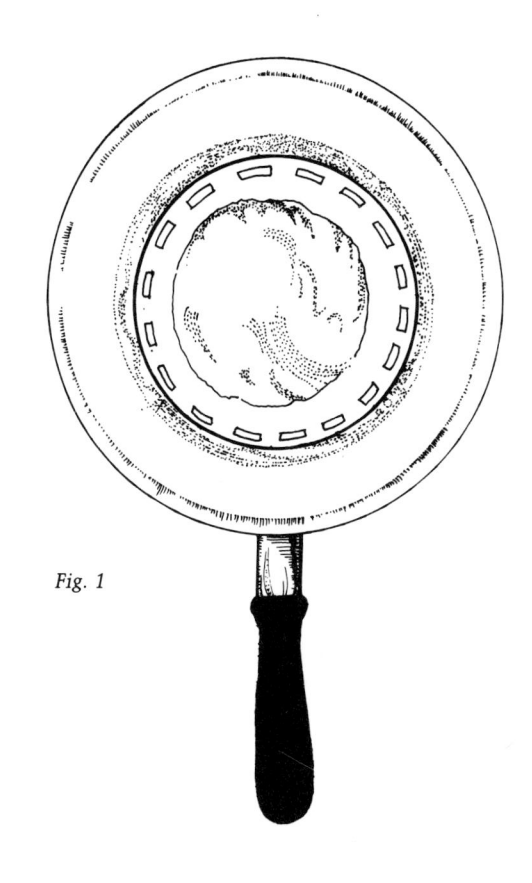

Fig. 1

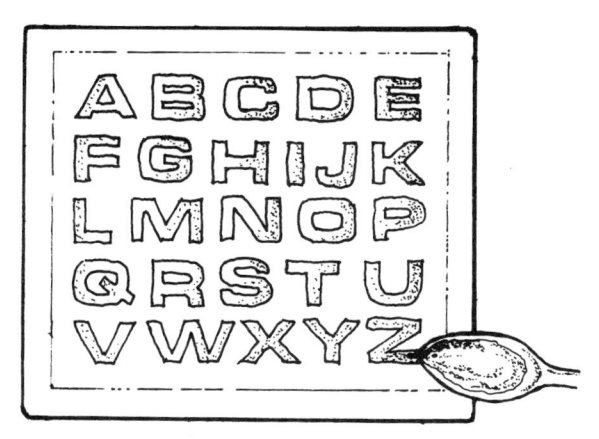

Fig. 2

Fig. 3

# Yellow Cakes

The four yellow cakes were designed to suit the beginner. The very simple designs can be made with either gum paste or silk flowers, plastic or gum paste bells.

## Yellow Cake with Cameo

*Step 1:* Mold the cameos (see page 16 for cameos). Set aside to dry.

*Step 2:* Cover the board with fondant following instructions on page 10, and let dry overnight. Cover the cake with fondant and place on the board. Pipe a leaf tip border around the base of the cake and let dry. *See figure 1.*

*Step 3:* Place a ribbon just above the piped border, and attach the lace piece just above the ribbon. *See figure 2.*

*Step 4:* Attach the cameo to the cake with royal icing and with a 0 tip, and royal icing to the count of 8, pipe a double row of beads around the cameo. *See figure 3.* Let dry.

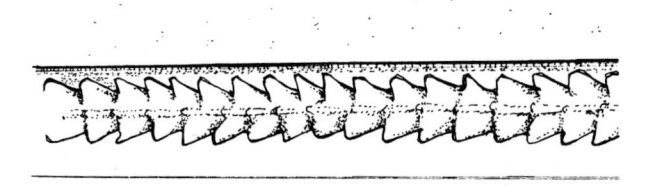

*Fig. 1*

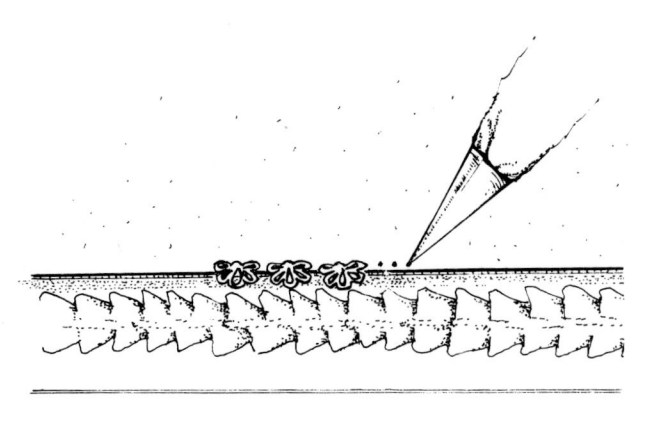

*Fig. 2*

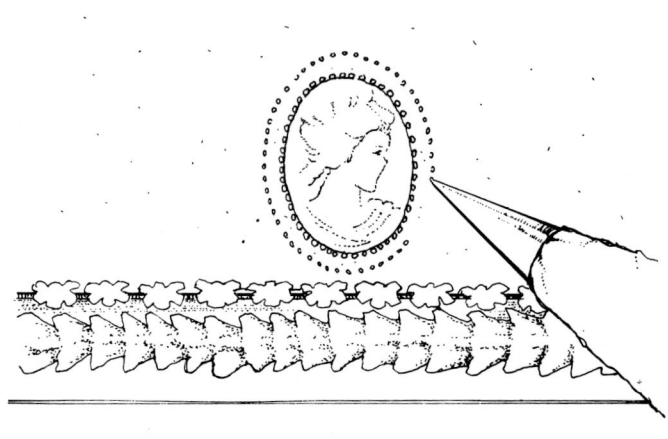

*Fig. 3*

## Yellow Cake with Basket

*Step 1:* Cover the board with fondant following instructions on page 10, and let dry overnight. Cover the cake with fondant and place on the board.

*Step 2:* Make the daisies from gum paste and place them into a flower former to dry. *See figure 1.*

*Step 3:* Lightly grease the basket mold. *See figure 2.* With a 0 or #1 tip, pipe the basket. *See figure 3.* Let dry. Make the roll by rolling out two very thin lengths of fondant. Roll the two together and with a small amount of icing, place the rope along the edge of the cake. *See figure 4.*

*Step 4:* Mark the cake with a template where the basket is to be placed. *See figure 5.* Pipe a small bead border around the basket, *see figure 6*, then place the basket on to the side of the cake. To allow the basket to dry on the cake without falling off, place a couple of hat pins into the cake. Let dry. Attach the daisies to the sides of the cake. *See figure 7.*

Fig. 1

Fig. 2

Fig. 3

Fig. 4

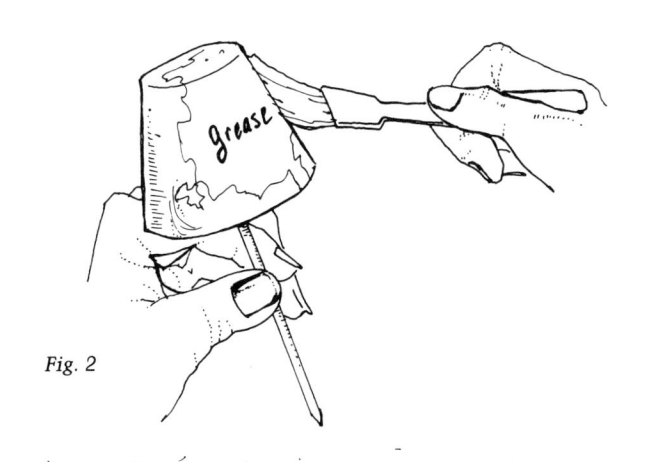

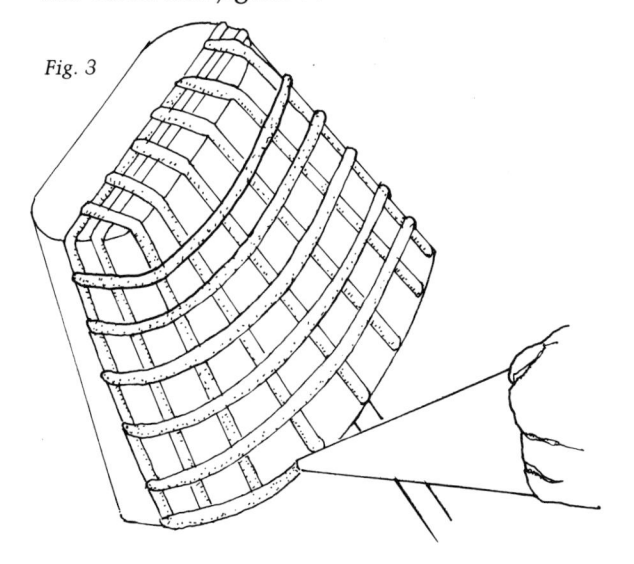

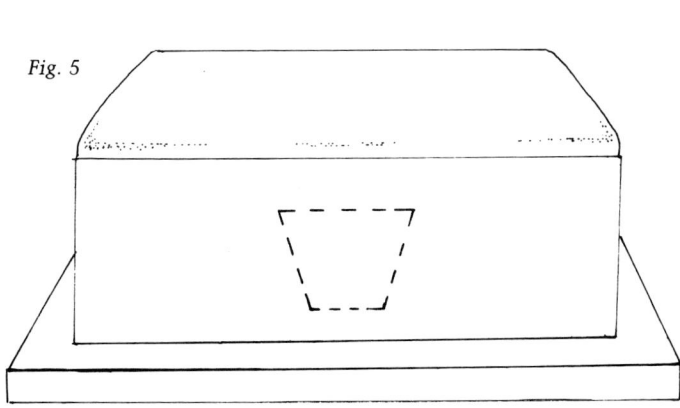

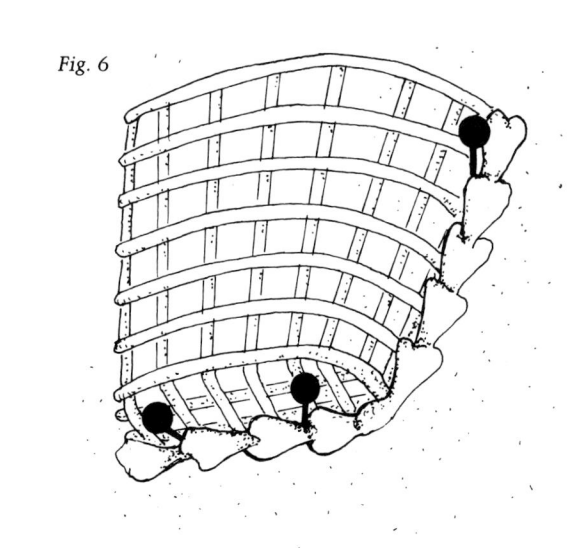

Fig. 5

Fig. 6

Fig. 7

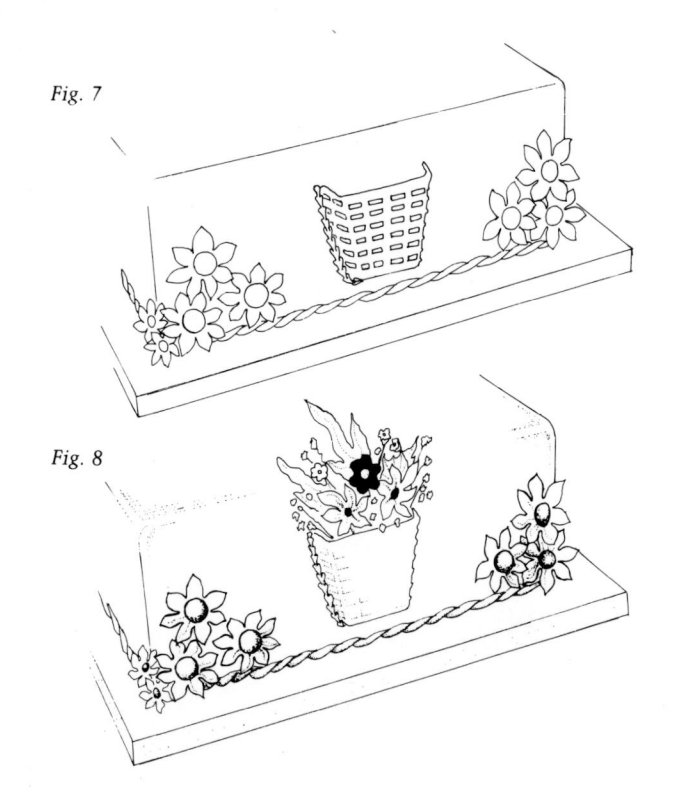

Fig. 8

Attach the daisies to the sides of the cake. *See figure 7.*

*Step 5:* Arrange a very small corsage of either silk or gum paste flowers to the cake behind the basket with royal icing, taking care not to break the basket. *See figure 8.*

## Yellow Cake with Embroidery

*Step 1:* Cover the board with fondant following instructions on page 10, and let dry overnight. Cover the cake with fondant and place on the board. While the fondant is still wet, press embroidery cutters into the corner of the cake.

*Step 2:* With a leaf tip, pipe a border with royal icing around the base of the cake.

*Step 3:* With either a 0 tip, or #1 tip, and royal icing to the count of 8, outline the embroidery cutters with small dots.

*Step 4:* With a 0 or #1 tip, pipe three small dots together on the side of the cake. Attach the ribbon and let dry. *See figure 1.*

Fig. 1

## Yellow Cake with Daisies

*Step 1:* Make gum paste daisies and place them into a flower former to dry.

*Step 2:* Cover the board with fondant following instructions on page 10, and let dry overnight. Cover the cake with fondant and place on the board. Pipe a leaf tip border around the base of the cake.

*Step 3:* With royal icing, attach the bells in the centre of the cake. *See figure 1.*

With royal icing, attach the daisies in the corner of the cake in groups of three. *See figure 2.* Let dry.

*Fig. 1*

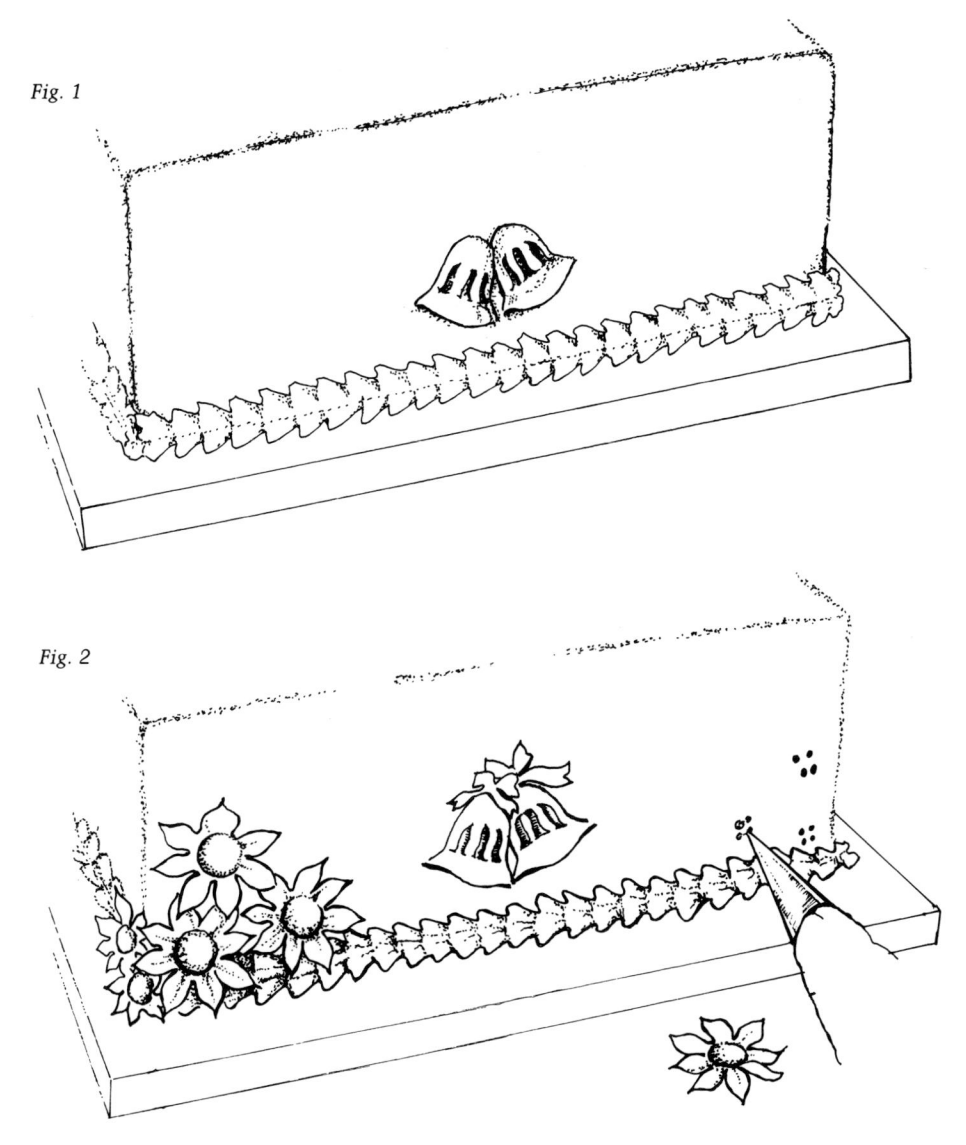

*Fig. 2*

# 3-Tier Art Decor

Many brides are today requesting black and white for wedding cakes, or a cake that does not resemble a traditional wedding cake.

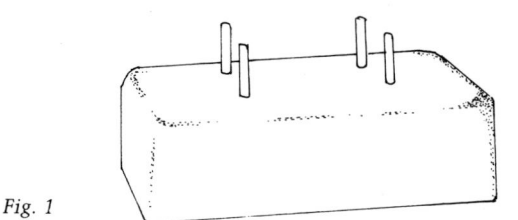

*Step 1:* Cover the board with black fondant following instructions on page 10, and let dry overnight. Cover the 3 cakes with fondant. Place the largest cake on the board and dowel the cake (see dowelling, page 14). *See figure 1.* Place the middle tier on top of the bottom cake and again dowel the middle cake. Place the top tier on top of the middle cake and with a #42 star tip, pipe around the bases of the three cakes and let dry.

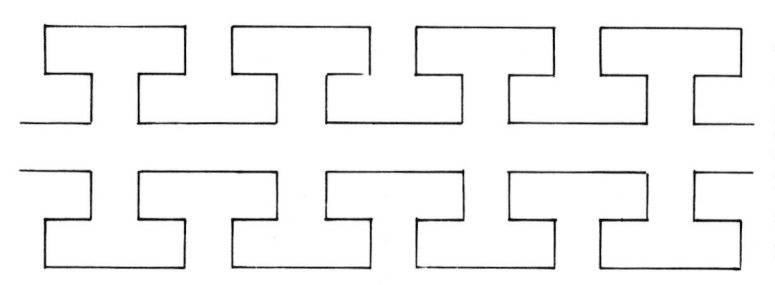

*Step 2:* Mark the pattern on the sides of each cake with a template. *See figure 2.* With a 0 or #1 tip, outline the pattern with a very small bead border on all 3 cakes. *See figure 3. Extreme* care must be taken when piping with black or any strong shade of food colours as any mistakes do not wipe off easily.

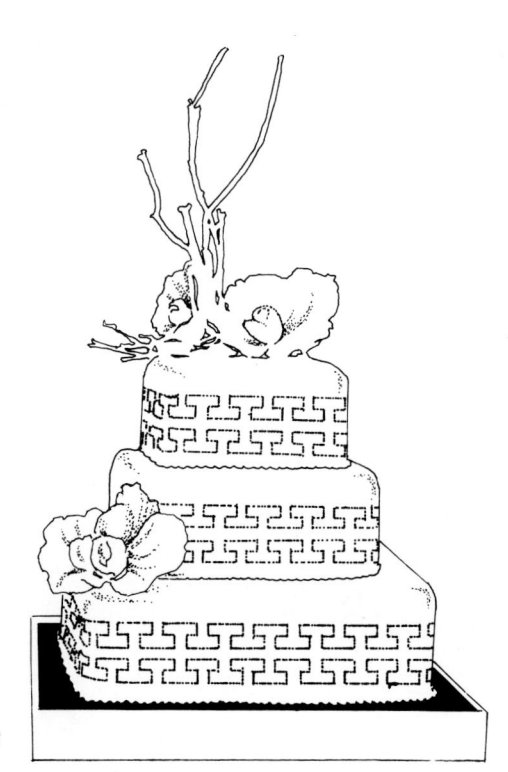

*Fig. 1*

*Fig. 2*

*Fig. 3*

# Intermediate

## Two-Tier Ruffle Cake

This elegant cake shows a different technique of using a ruffle.

*Step 1:* Cover the boards with fondant following instructions on page 10, and let dry overnight. Cover the cakes with fondant and place on the boards. With a #2 tip, pipe a small bead border around the base of the cake and let dry overnight.

*Step 2:* Cut sections of fondant (to which gum trag has been added) with the frill cutter. Cut off the scalloped edge to form a straight edge frill. Place the frill on a dusted cornstarch board and with an anger tool, ruffle both edges. *See figure 1.* Dust off excess cornstarch. With a #2 tip, pipe royal icing along the centre of the ruffle. *See figure 2.* Attach to the cake, and continue applying the sections until the cake is completed.

*Step 3:* Cut out the top ruffle, this time making the ruffle 1/2" (13 mm) narrower in width. Ruffle both edges. Apply the top ruffle with royal icing. This time when seaming the pieces together, pipe a small section of icing down the centre of both seams and smooth with a palette knife. *See figure 3.*

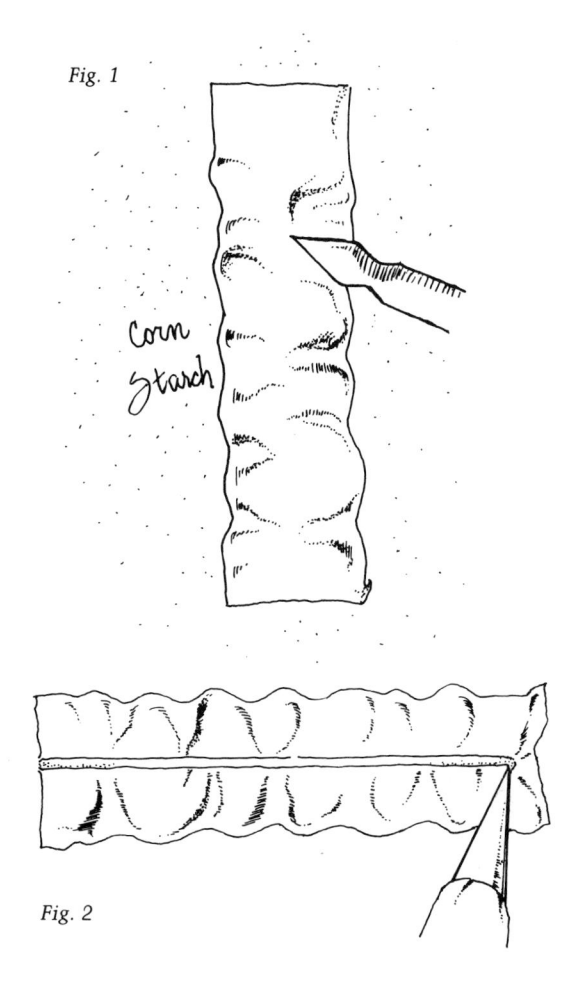

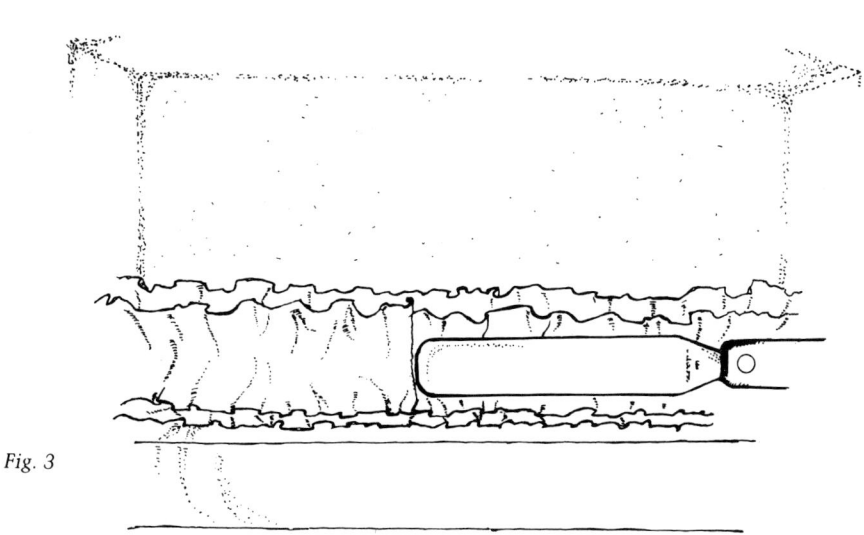

Fig. 1

Fig. 2

Fig. 3

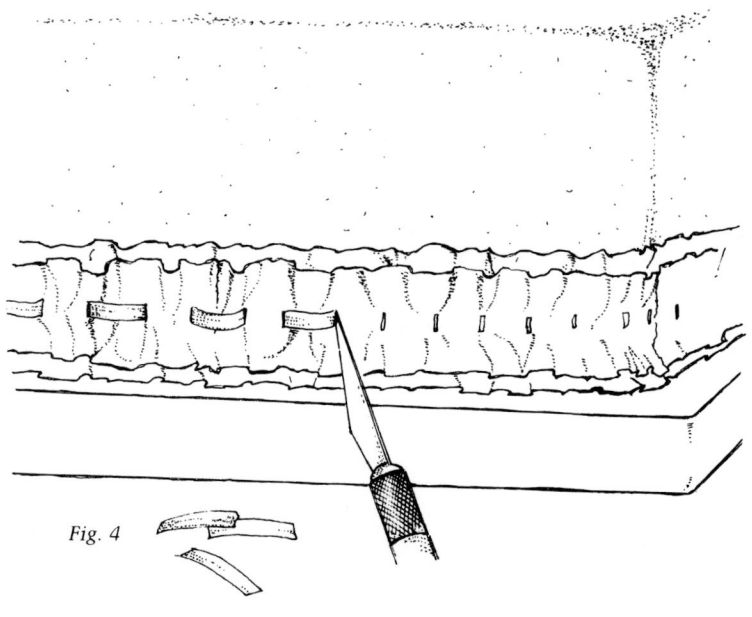

*Step 4:* Using an Xacto knife, cut small slits through the fondant, approximately 1/2" (13 mm) apart, all around the cake to allow for placement of the ribbon. Cut small sections of ribbon (to be inserted into the slits on the cake), making sure they are all the same length, but slightly longer than the width between the slits to allow the ribbon ends to tuck easily into the slits. *See figure 4.*

*Step 5:* Mark embroidery and pipe with a 0 tip and let dry. Repeat for top tier.

Fig. 4

Fig. 1

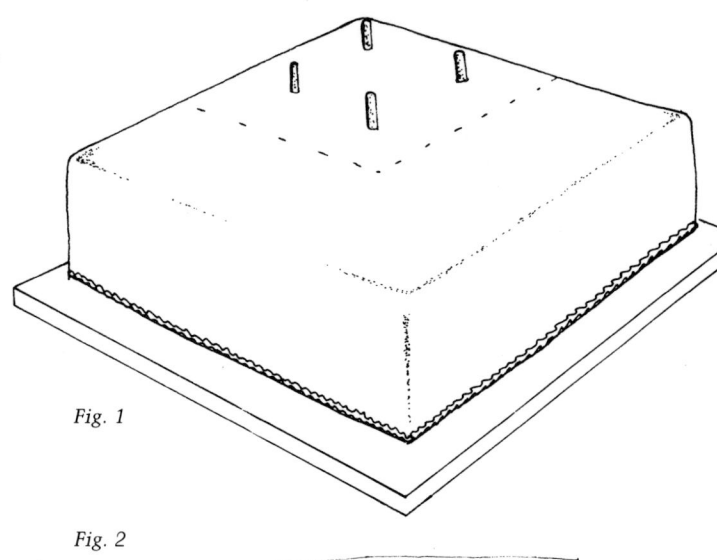

Fig. 2

## Two-Tier Beige Cake

This cake combines both brush embroidery and filigree attached directly to the sides of the cake. The design of the brush work can be changed to correspond with the flowers, i.e. orchids, carnations, tulips and a favourite of mine, calla lilies.

*Step 1:* Cover the board with fondant following instructions on page 10, and let dry overnight. Cover both cakes with fondant and attach the largest cake to the board. With a #2 tip, pipe a small bead border around the base of the cake.

*Step 2:* Dowel the area where the smaller cake will sit, following instructions on page 14. *See figure 1.* Attach the top tier, and with a #2 tip, pipe a small bead border around the base of the cake. Let dry.

*Step 3:* Draw your pattern to the height of your cakes. Place the pattern on to a plexiglass square, and cover the pattern with either a cooking film or a soft plastic. With a #2 tip and royal icing, brush the flower and leaves in (see brush work, step 4, 2 tier cake page 34). With a #0 tip, pipe the filigree in ,and with royal icing to a count of 10, flood the solid line in. *See figure 2.* Let dry overnight or longer. To release the brush work, very carefully turn the work over and very gently peel the cooking film from the piped pieces.

*Step 4:* With a 0 tip, pipe a small bead border along the back inside of the filigree work and attach to both corners of the cake. Let dry. *See figure 3*. With a 0 tip, pipe a small bead border down the centre seam of the two adjoining filigree pieces. *See figure 4*. Repeat until all pieces are attached to the cake. Let dry. *See figure 5*.

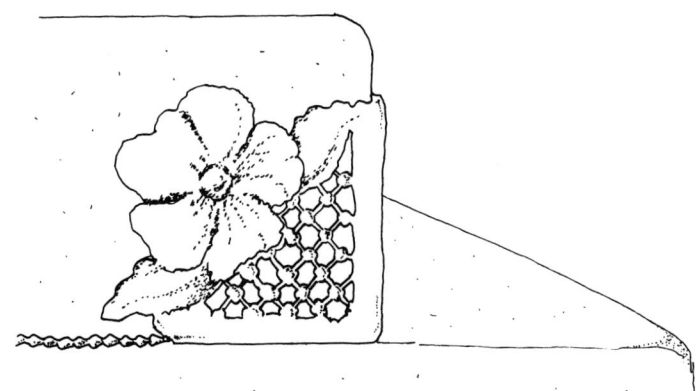

Fig. 3

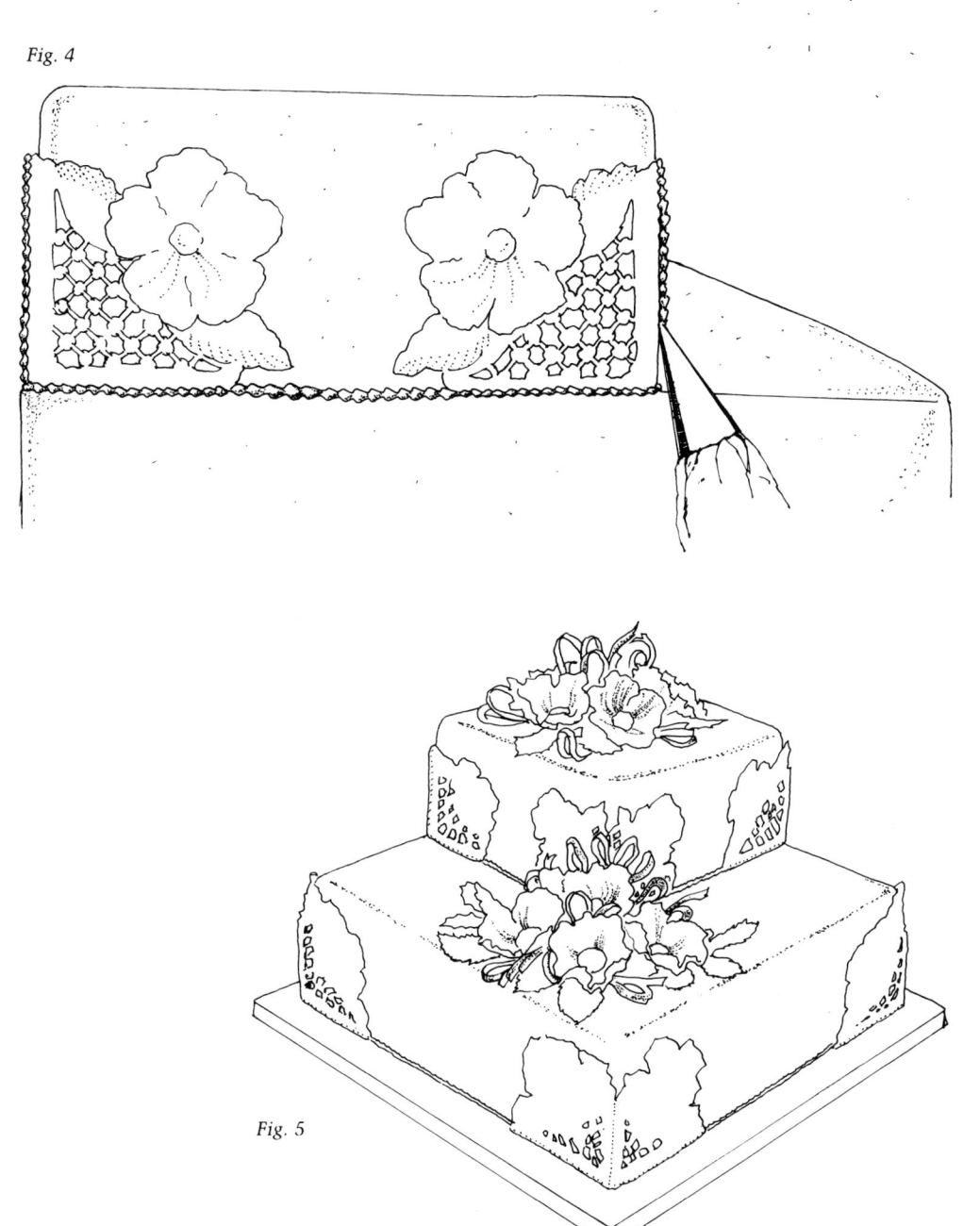

Fig. 4

Fig. 5

*Fig. 1*

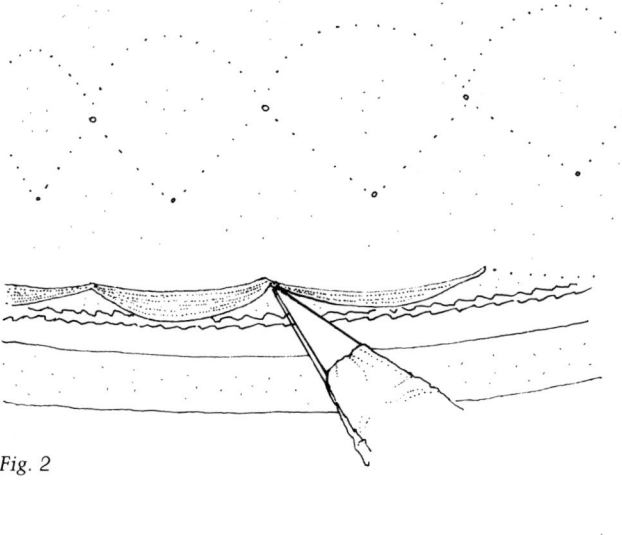

*Fig. 2*

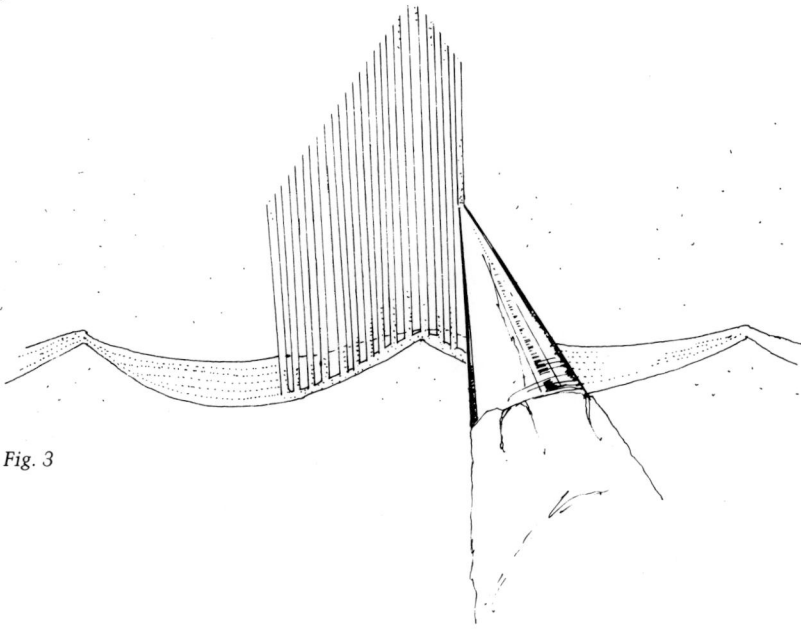

*Fig. 3*

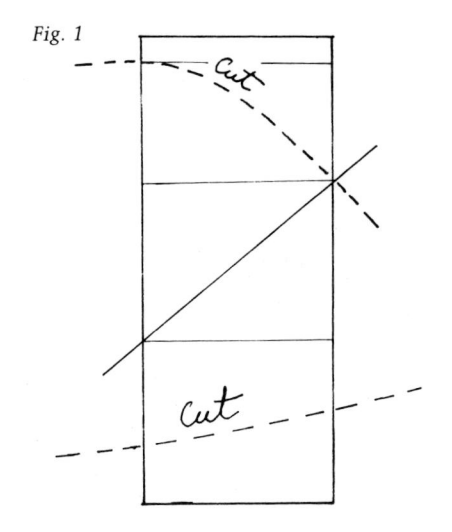

# Blue One-Tier Cake

A very pretty way to compliment the use of lace pieces.

*Step 1:* Cover the board with fondant following instructions on page 10, and let dry overnight. Cover the cake with fondant and place on the board. With a #2 tip, pipe a small bead border around the base of the cake and let dry.

*Step 2:* Make a false collar and place it around the cake making sure the collar is almost touching the board. Mark the pattern on the side of the cake. *See figure 1.*

*Step 3:* With a #2 tip, pipe the scallop bridging for 6 lines (first line all the way around), 2nd, 3rd, 4th and 5th lines graduate 1/8" (3 mm) from both ends, allowing each line to dry before attempting the next line. The 6th line must go all the way around. Let dry. *See figure 2.* With colour flow to the count of 10, colour flow the bridging. This both strengthens and hides the bridge work. Let dry 4 hours.

*Step 4:* With a 0 tip, pipe the strings down from the lower line which will automatically form the points of the pattern. *See figure 3.* Let dry while making lace pieces.

*Step 5:* When dry, attach lace pieces by applying small dots of icing to the cake and attaching the lace pieces. When applying the lace pieces to the points, always attach the top two lace pieces to either sides of the points, then down the sides of the points. *See figure 4.* Lastly, attach the lace pieces on to the marked arch and let dry.

*Fig. 4*

*Step 6:* With a 0 tip, mark the top embroidery and let dry. With a 0 tip, pipe small scallops around the base of the string work and let dry.

*Step 7:* Roll out gum-paste very thin and cut out small blossoms. Place the blossoms on a small piece of foam or sponge, and with a metal ball tool, cup the petals towards the centre of the flower. Attach to the cake with royal icing and let dry. *See figure 5.*

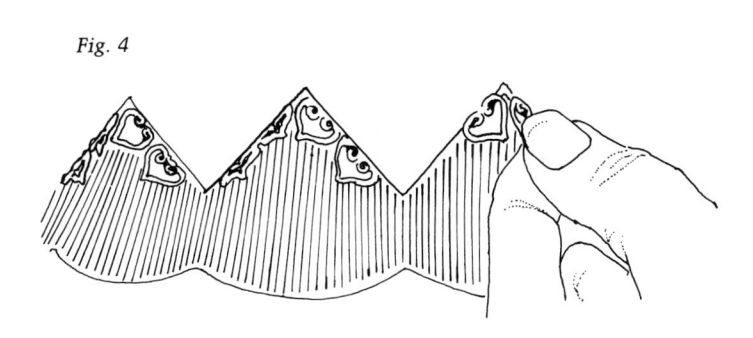

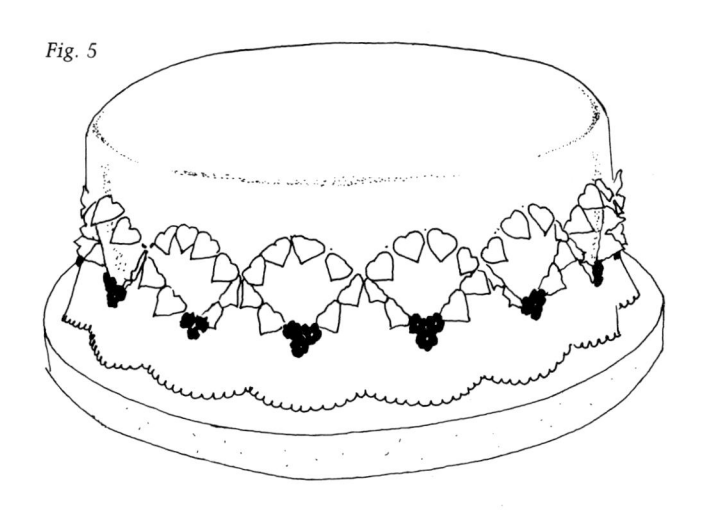

*Fig. 5*

# Advanced

## Two-Tier Yellow Cake

This elegant cake combines both brush embroidery and layered stringwork.

The design for brush embroidery can be changed to match the flowers on top of the cake.

*Step 1:* First trace the pattern of the flowers on a small piece of soft cardboard (the cardboard should be the same height as the cake). With a #1 tip, pipe the pattern and set aside to dry (keep these "embossed cards" for future use).

*Step 2:* Cover the boards with fondant following instructions on page 10, and let dry overnight. Cover the cakes with fondant and place on the boards. While the fondant is still soft, take the embossed cards and press the cards into the side of the cake where you would like the patterns to be. With a #2 tip, pipe a small bead border around the base of the cake and let dry.

*Step 3:* Make a false collar and place around the cake. *See figure 1.* Mark the pattern on the side

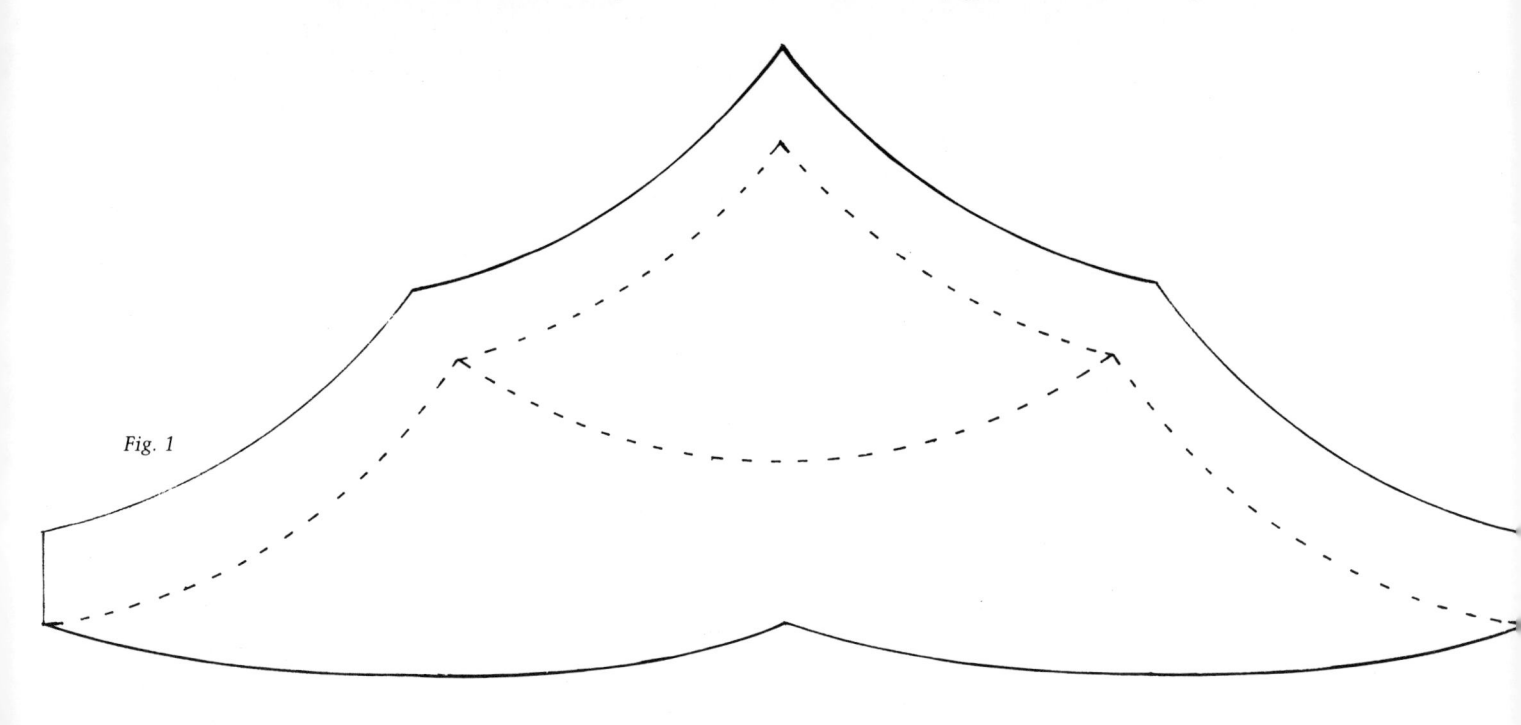

*Fig. 1*

of the cake. With a #2 tip, pipe the lowest bridging, let dry, then flood in the bridging and let dry.

*Step 4:* Complete the brush embroidery. With a #2 tip and royal icing, outline *only* one petal at a time, then with a #5 soft brush and a small bowl of water or lemon juice, dampen the brush and from the top of the petal, stroke down and inwards from the sides of the petal to the centre of the flower. Care must be taken that the complete petal has the sugar mixture applied (do not use more water than required). Continue until the flower has been completed, then with a #1 tip, pipe the stamens in the centre of the flower and let dry.

*Step 5:* With a 0 tip, pipe the string from the third marked line on the side of the cake to the bridging at the base of the cake and let dry. *See figure 2.* Repeat the bridging for the middle bridge, only this time pipe only 3 lines for this bridge. Let dry, flood in again and let dry. Pipe strings. Let dry. *See figure 3.* Finally, pipe the last bridging all around the cake, this time piping 2 lines for the bridging and let dry. Again, repeat piping the string with a 0 tip and let dry. *See figure 4.* With a 0 tip, pipe all the scallops around the edges of the string work. *See figure 5.* Mark and pipe the embroidery just above the strings and let dry. Repeat for top tier. *See figure 6.*

*Fig. 2*

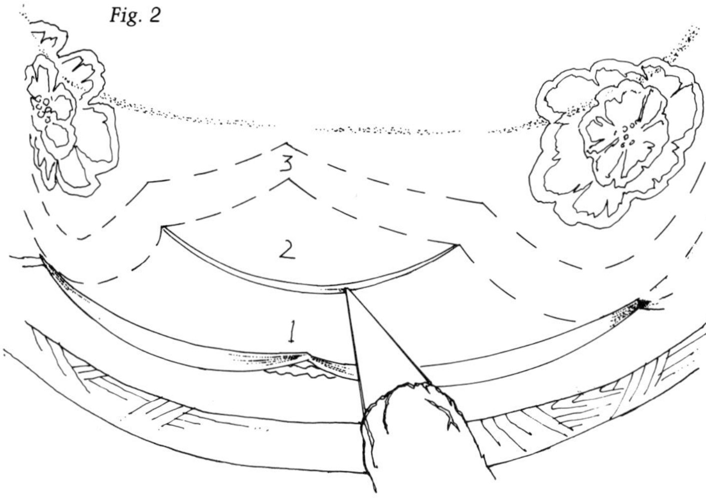

*Fig. 3*

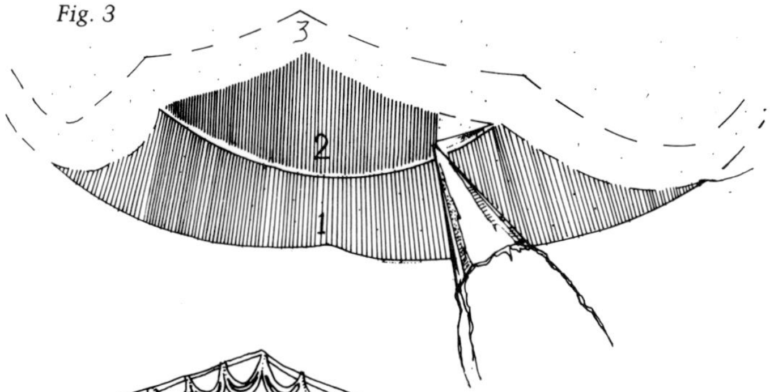

*Fig. 4*

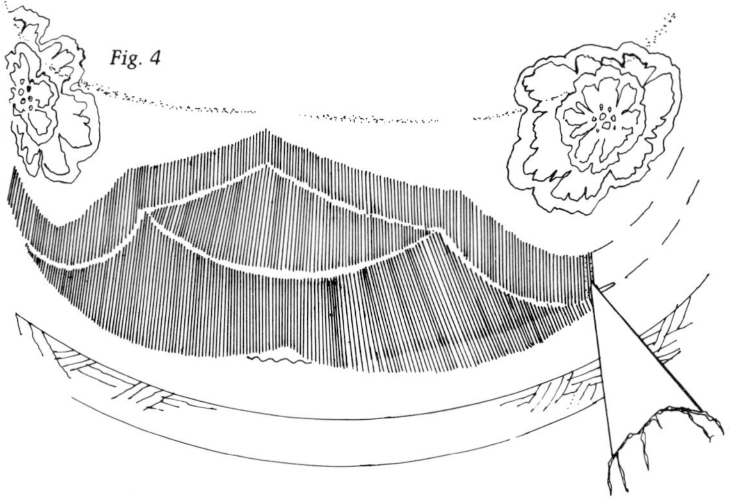

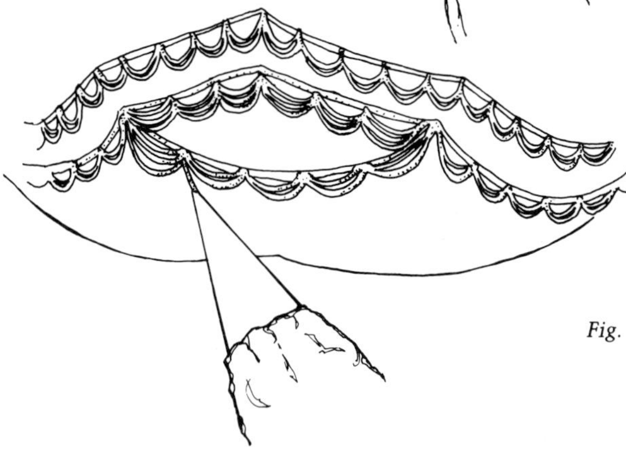

*Fig. 5*

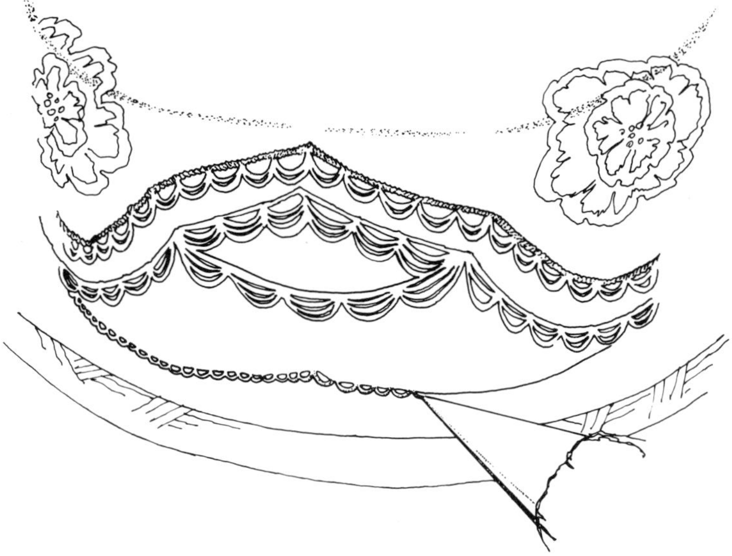

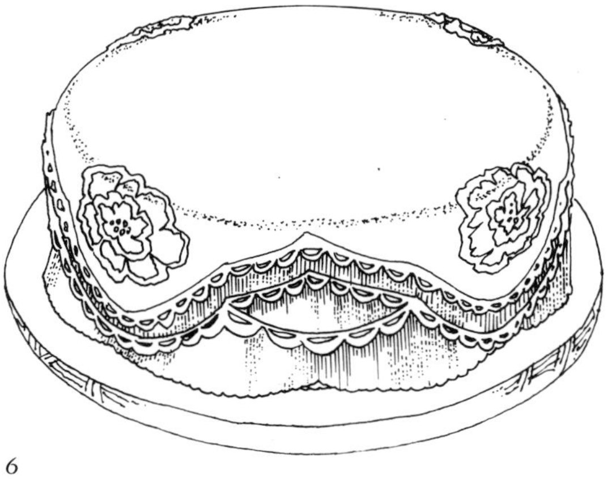

*Fig. 6*

*Fig. 1*

*Fig. 2* False Collar

*Fig. 3*

*Fig. 4*

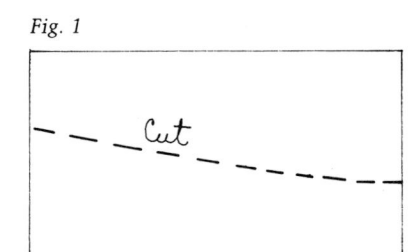

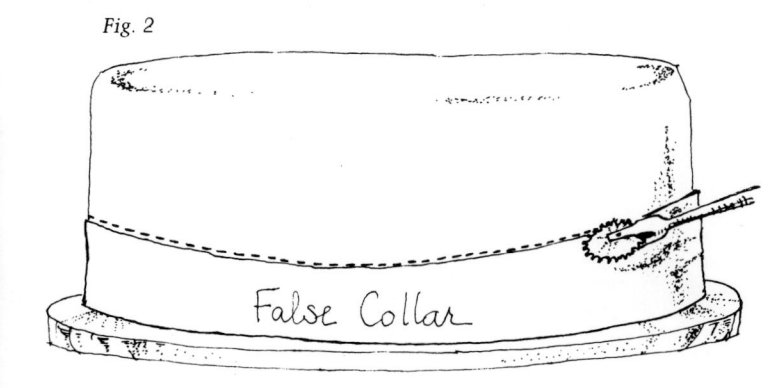

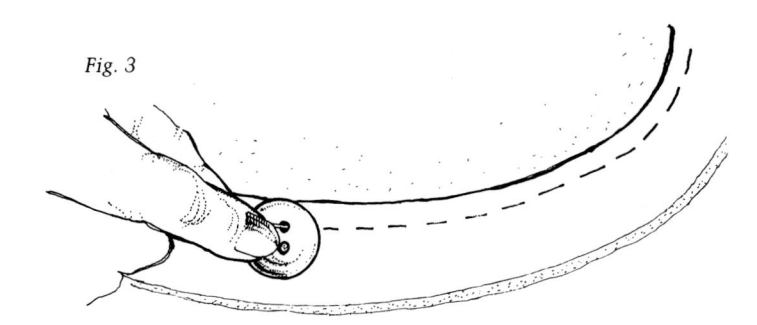

## Two-Tier Oval Cake

This elegant cake combines lace and ruffles together with the touch of a cameo.

*Step 1:* Cover the boards with fondant following instructions on page 10, and let dry overnight. Cover the cakes with fondant and place on the boards, and with a #2 tip pipe a small bead border around the base of the cakes. Let dry.

*Step 2:* Mold the cameo following instructions on page 16, and let dry.

*Step 3:* Make a false collar and cut to the style required and attach around the cake. *See figure 1*. Attach the collar so that it fits on to the board. With a dressmaker's wheel, outline the top section of the pattern. *See figure 2.* Use a button with a toothpick inserted through the centre, mark the base of the cake on the board (see Two-Tier White Cake for marking boards, page 62). *See figure 3.*

*Step 4:* With a #2 tip, pipe a solid line around the marked line on the board and also pipe a solid line on to the side of the cake. Let dry. With a 0 tip, pipe the strings from the top marked line down to the lower marked line of the board. *See figure 4.* Let dry.

*Step 5:* Roll out fondant and cut out a straight frill approximately 3/4" (19 mm) wide and ruffle one edge. Pipe a line of royal icing along the base

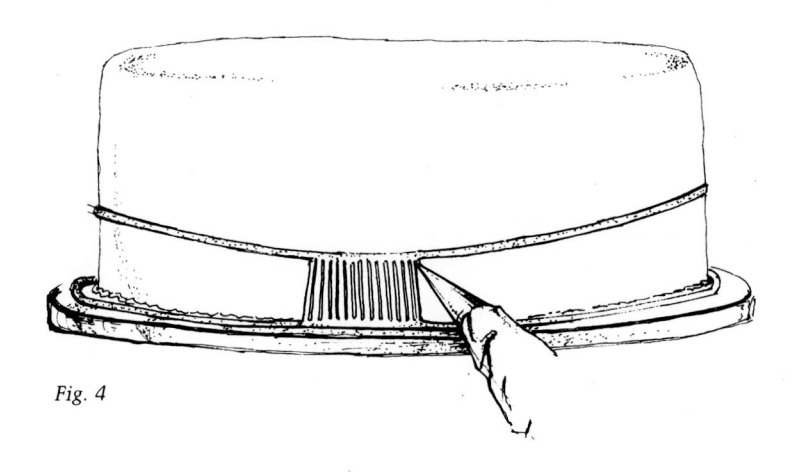

Two-Tier Ruffle Cake

Two-Tier Beige Cake

**BLUE ONE-TIER CAKE**

TWO-TIER YELLOW CAKE

TWO-TIER OVAL CAKE

of the straight edge of the ruffle and attach at the top line of the strings. *See figure 5*. Repeat, attaching the 2nd ruffle. Let dry. When dry, very carefully dust the edges of the dry ruffles with dusting powder. To give the effect of netting, pipe little dots all over the cake with a 0 tip. *See figure 6*. With royal icing to a count of 8, and a 0 tip, pipe dots on every other string. *See figure 7*.

*Step 6:* For the ruffle around the cameo, roll fondant out and cut out a straight ruffle. Ruffle around one edge and with a small amount of icing, attach the frill to the cameo then on to the cake. *See figure 8*.

*Step 7:* Make lace pieces with a 0 tip and let dry at least 4 hours. Attach the lace pieces around the cameo and let dry. *See figure 9*. To neaten the base of the strings, attach a very narrow ribbon around the base of the cake. Repeat for top tier.

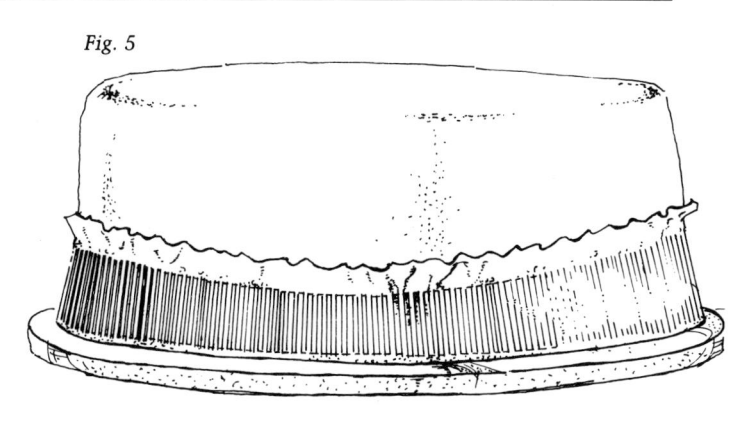

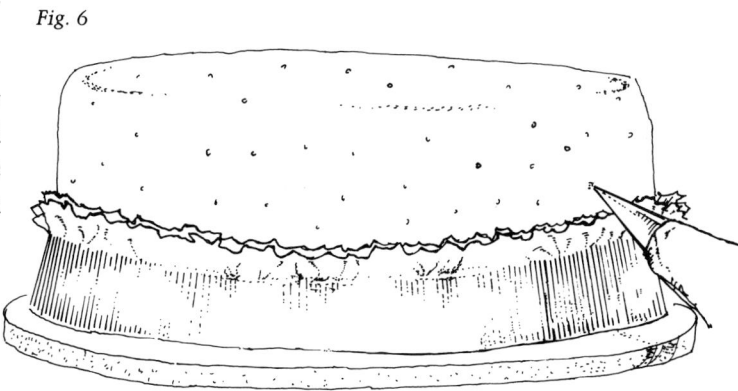

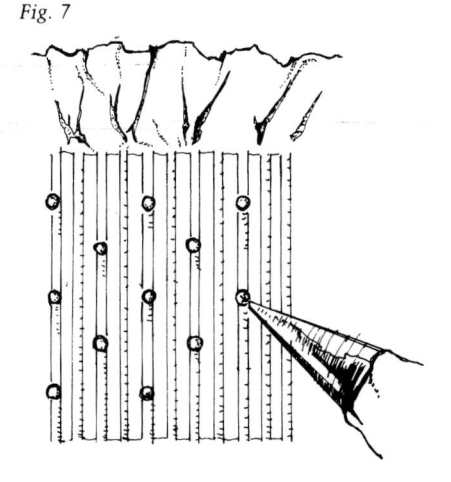

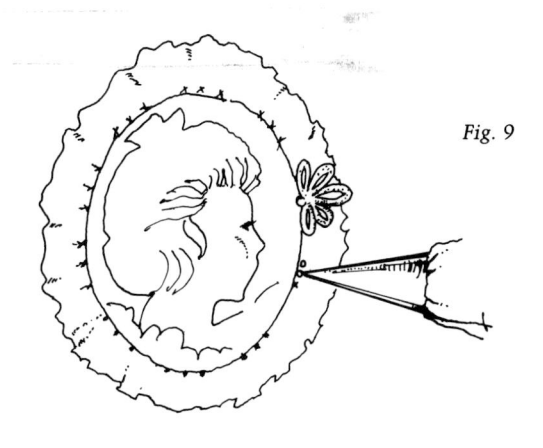

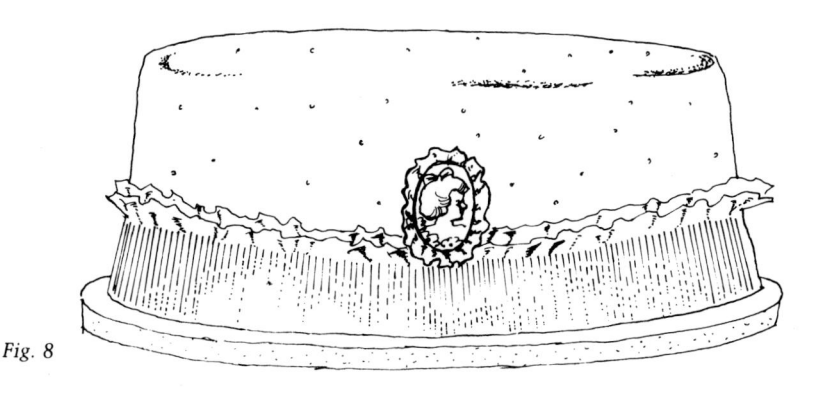

Fig. 5

Fig. 6

Fig. 7

Fig. 9

Fig. 8

*Fig. 1*

*Fig. 2*

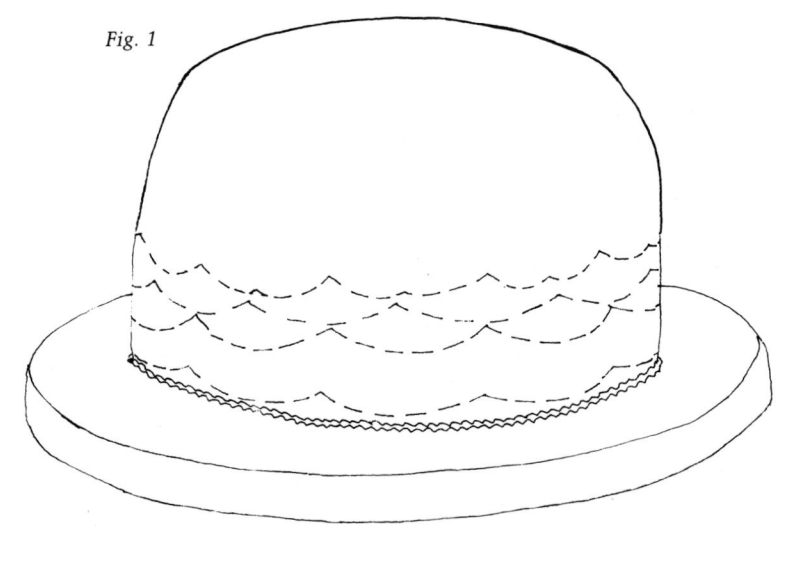

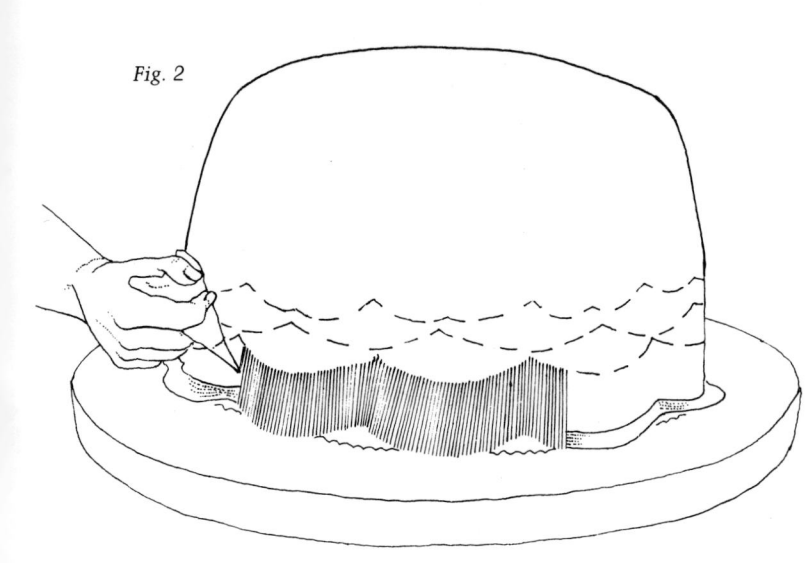

## Blue Cake—
## Double String Work

This cake combines both double and layered stringwork.

*Step 1:* Cover the board with fondant following instructions on page 10, and let dry overnight. Cover the cake with fondant and place on the board. With a #2 tip, pipe a small bead border around the base of the cake, and let dry 2 hours. Make a false collar and attach to the cake, marking the pattern on the sides of the cake. *See figure 1.*

*Step 2:* With a #2 tip, pipe the bridging on the lowest bridge only. Let dry. Flood the bridge in with a dark shade of icing. Again let dry at least 4 hours. With a 0 tip, and a dark shade of icing, pipe the strings from the middle marked line to the bridge. Continue all around the cake and let dry. *See figure 2.*

*Step 3:* Extend the bridging, this time using a lighter shade of icing (this work is called double stringwork). Again flood in, taking care not to break any of the first strings and let dry at least 4 hours. With a 0 tip, and a lighter shade of icing, pipe the string from just above the first strings to the new bridging, and continue all around the cake. Let dry.

*Step 4:* With a #2 tip, repeat the bridging, this time piping 4 lines directly on top of the edge of the first set of strings. Let dry, flood in and let dry at least 4 hours.

*Step 5:* Repeat piping strings with a 0 tip from the 2nd marked line to the new bridge. Let dry. Repeat the bridging, this time pipe 3 lines with a #2 tip. Let dry. With a 0 tip, pipe the last set of strings and let dry. *See figure 3.*

*Step 6:* Pipe a scallop around the base of the strings and a picot at the very top edge of the first strings. *See figure 4.* Let dry. Attach the cherub molds with royal icing. Make lace pieces and let dry.

*Step 7:* Attach the lace pieces around the cherub molds. Let dry.
*(See page 15 for instructions on filet crochet)*

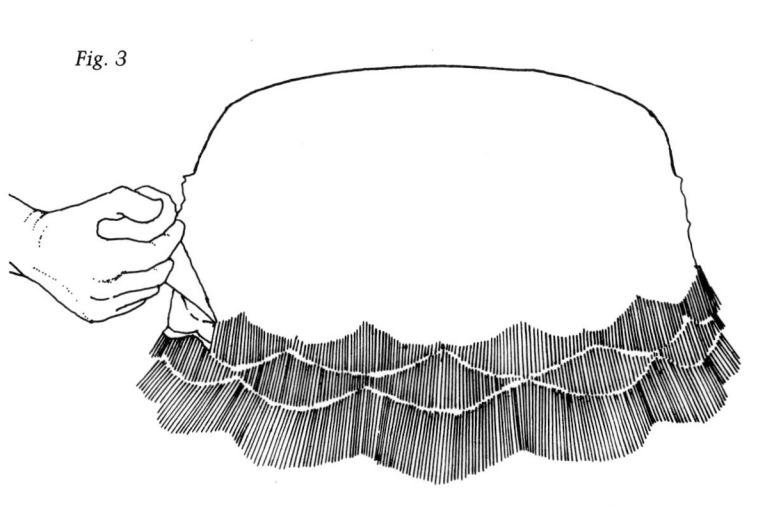

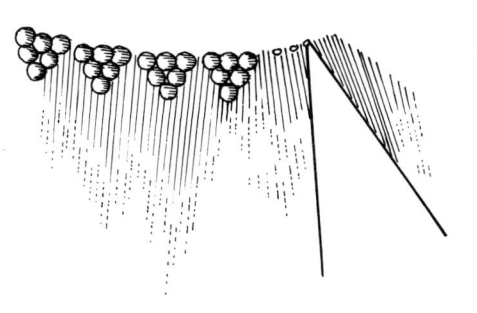

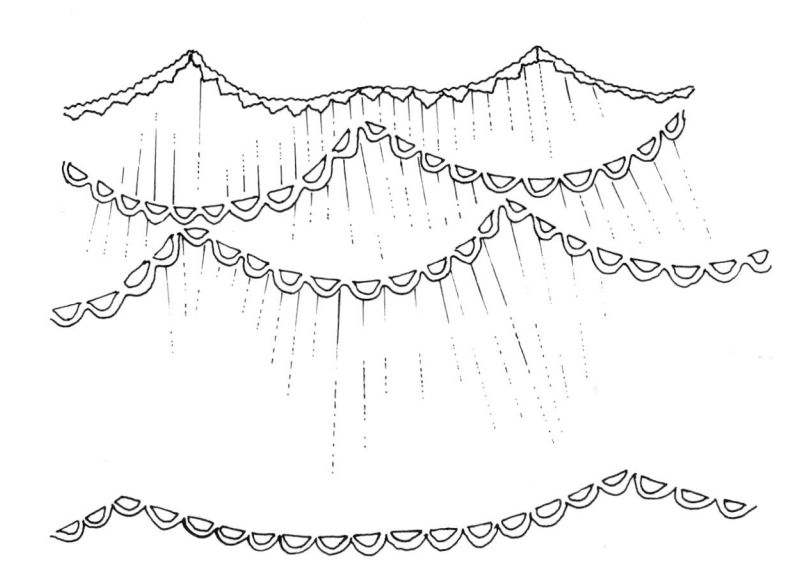

Fig. 3

Fig. 4

# New Techniques

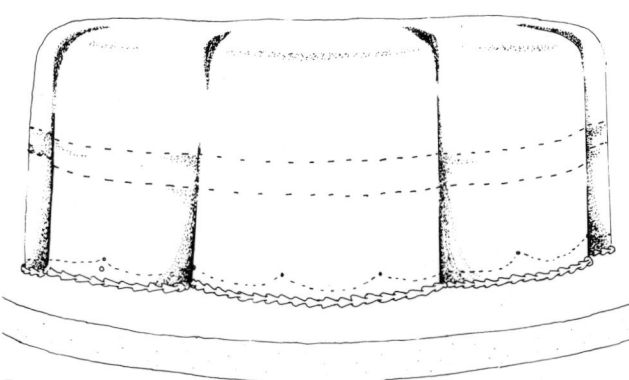

*Fig. 1*

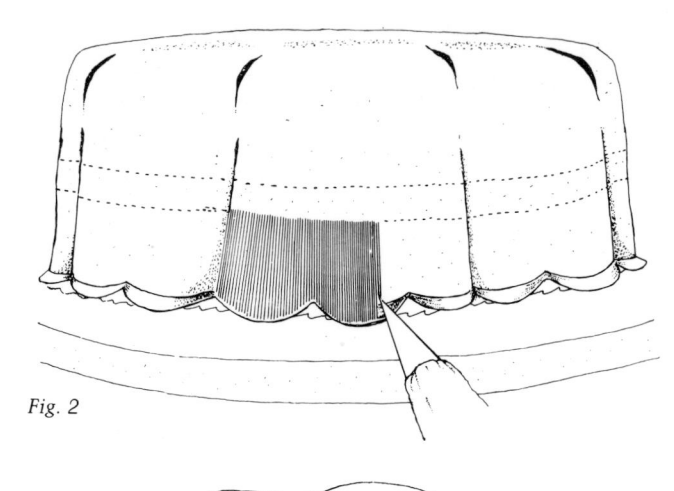

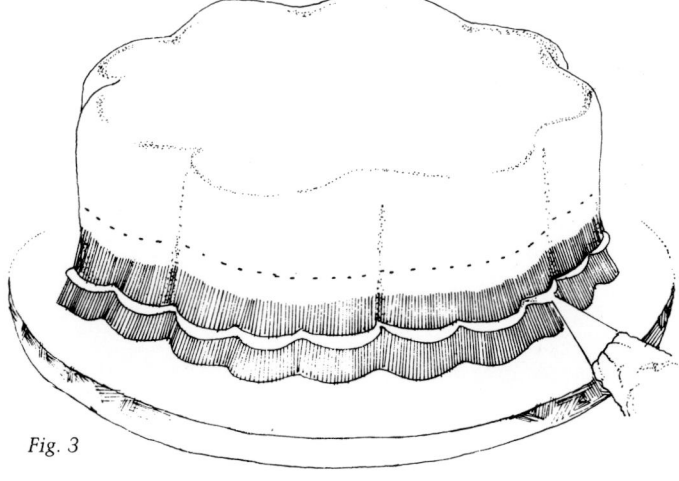

*Fig. 2*

*Fig. 3*

## Anniversary Cake

This cake in varied shades of yellow is probably the most difficult cake to decorate. The technique used is layered stringwork and open bridging.

*Step 1:* Cover the board with the darkest shade of yellow fondant following instructions on page 10 and let dry overnight. Cover the cake with a very soft shade of yellow fondant and place on the board. With a #2 tip, pipe a small bead border around the base of the cake and let dry.

*Step 2:* Make a number "50" (see Figure 10 for pattern) using the "Floodwork" instructions on page 16.

*Step 3:* Make a false collar to fit the cake and mark two solid lines around the middle of the cake with a dressmaker's wheel. *See figure 1.* Pipe the bridging with a #2 tip. Let dry. Flood in the bridging with a dark shade of royal icing and let dry 4 hours (or longer).

*Step 4:* With a 0 tip, pipe strings from the lowest line attaching the strings to the bridging. Continue all the way around the cake and let dry 4 hours. *See figure 2.* Once dry, with a #2 tip, pipe a scallop approximately half way up the strings, and when you have piped one scallop all the way around the cake, pipe two more scallops on top of the first scallop and let dry. *See figure 3.* When dry, pipe with a #2 tip from the centre of the scallop to the centre of the next scallop. (You may have to tilt the cake slightly forward so that the scallop does not sag). Let dry. *See figure 4.* With royal icing to the count of 10, flood in the dry 3 lines of scallop with a lighter shade of yellow. Extra care must be taken when flooding as the back strings cannot be repaired if they are broken. Let dry. With a 0 tip, pipe strings from the top marked line to the new bridging. Let dry. *See figure 5.*

*Step 5:* When dry, with a 0 tip, pipe two lines of scallops around the top of the strings. *See figure 6.* Then pipe a small scallop around the lower edges of the strings. *See figure 7.* Then pipe a small upside down "C" directly on to the very edge of the strings. Let dry. *See figure 8.*

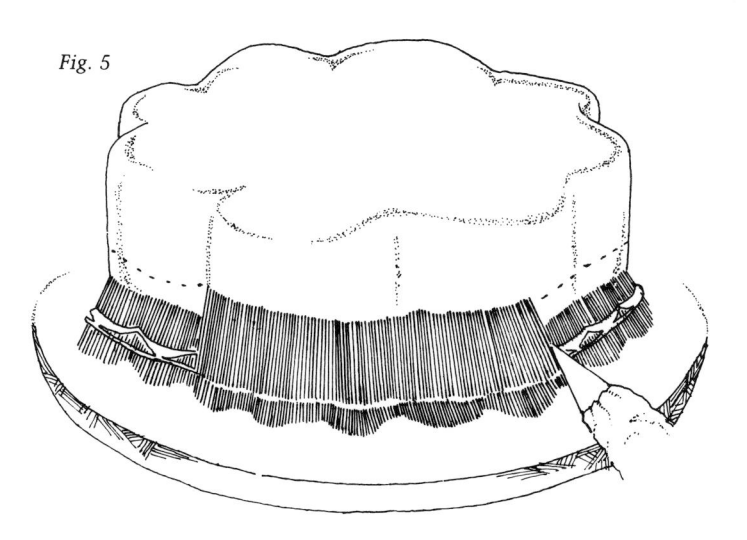

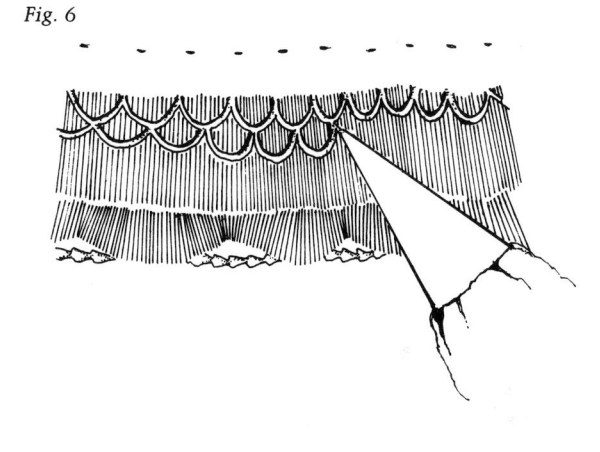

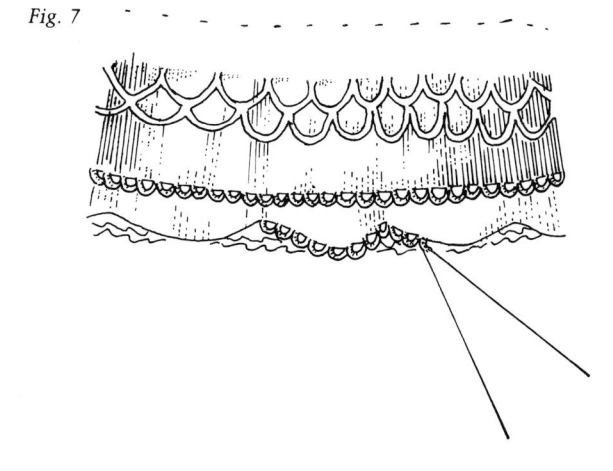

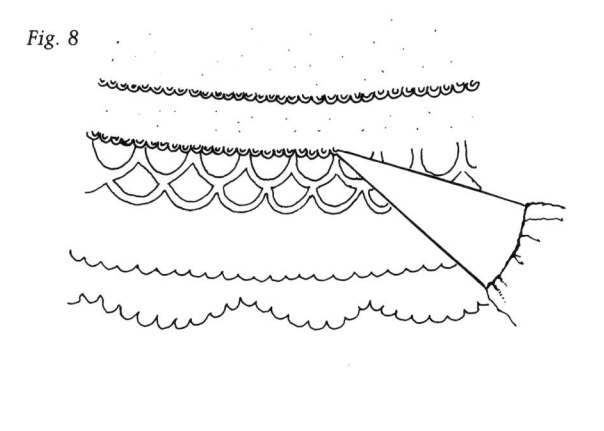

Fig. 4

Fig. 5

Fig. 6

Fig. 7

Fig. 8

46 *New Techniques*

*Step 6:* Attach the ribbon with royal icing. Mark and pipe embroidery with a 0 tip and let dry.

*Step 7:* Attach the number "50" on top of the cake with royal icing then paint the "50" with a gold food colour dust. *See figure 9.*

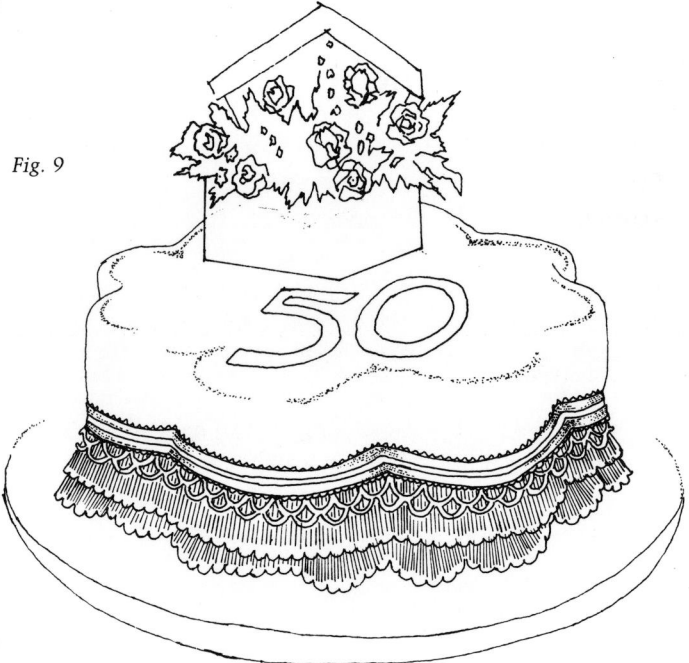

*Fig. 9*

*Fig. 10*

## Anniversary Music Box

*Step 1:* Cut out the pieces of the box, *see figure 11*, from pastillage (see page 9). Place the pieces on a flat surface to dry. (If the pieces are very large, turn them frequently to prevent buckling). Cut a hole in one of the side pieces to enable the handle of the music box to fit through. Leave to dry at least 24 hours.

*Step 2:* When dry, sand the edges of the pieces with fine sandpaper. With a #1 tip, attach the pieces together using royal icing. Pipe inside the box to give added strength and let dry. Place a layer of royal icing on to the base of the music insert and sit the insert in the bottom of the box. Pipe with a #1 tip around the insert to strengthen and let dry overnight.

*Step 3:* Fill the empty space of the box with either foam or florist oasis and arrange the flowers in the foam.

*Step 4:* Attach the lid using a #1 tip and royal icing and keep the lid propped open until dry. Paint with gold food colour and place on top of the cake.

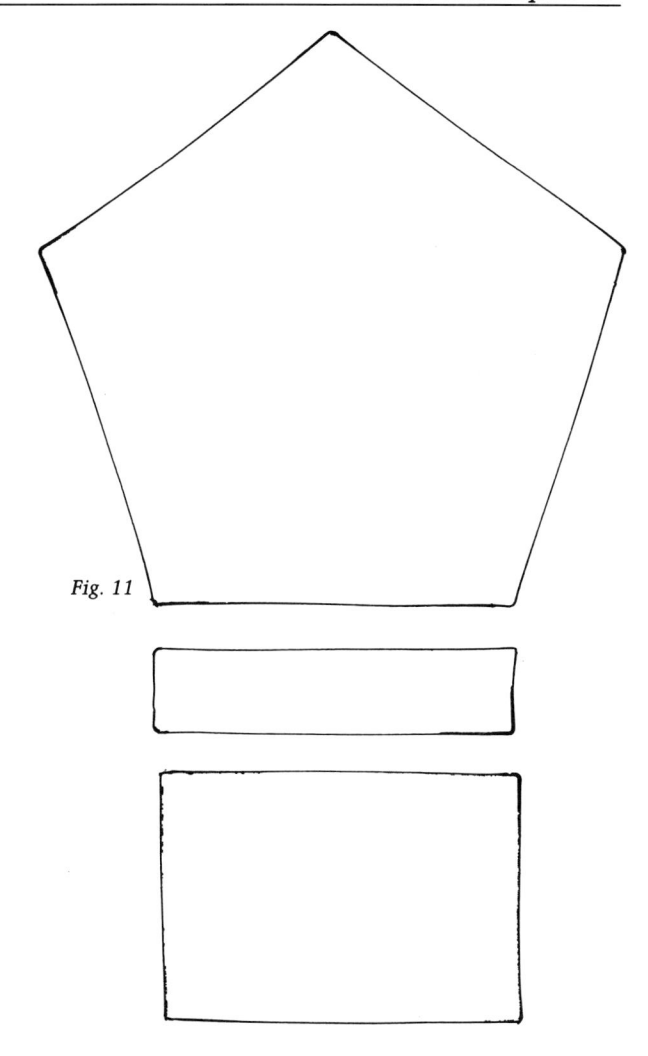

*Fig. 11*

## Dutch Iris

Tape a 22g wire with green florist tape and make a very small hook on one end. Take a small piece of gum-paste (the same shade as the flower) and make a three-sided straight bud approximately ³/₄" (2cm) in length. Dip the hook wire into gum glue and push through the centre of the bud. Dry overnight. *See figure 1*.

Roll out gum-paste very thinly, and cut out 3 petals. Thin the top half of the petal with a pewter tool (to give a curly effect). *See figure 2*. Fold the petal in half lengthwise to create a crease effect, then vein. With crease side facing you, paint gum glue to one side of the dried, three-sided bud and attach the petal. *See figure 3*. Continue until all three petals have been

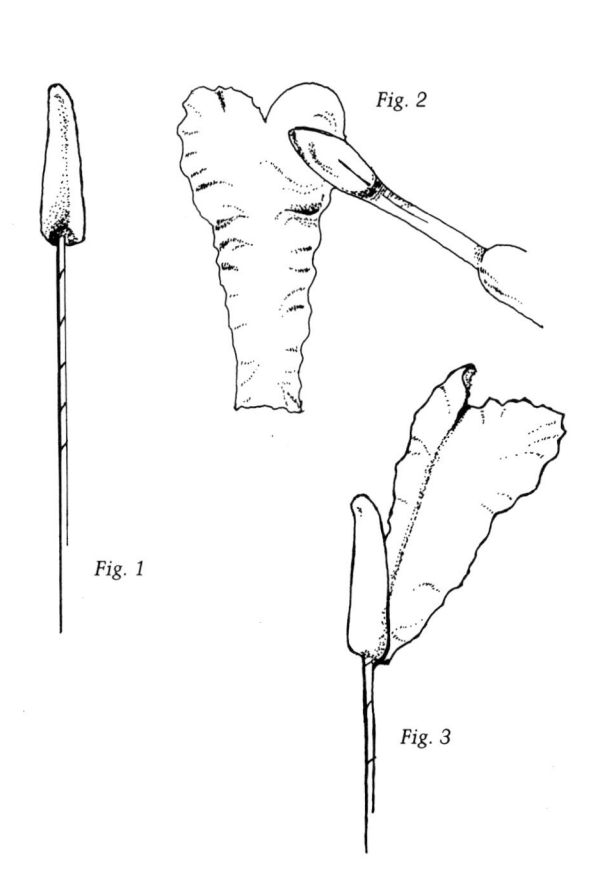

*Fig. 1*

*Fig. 2*

*Fig. 3*

48  New Techniques

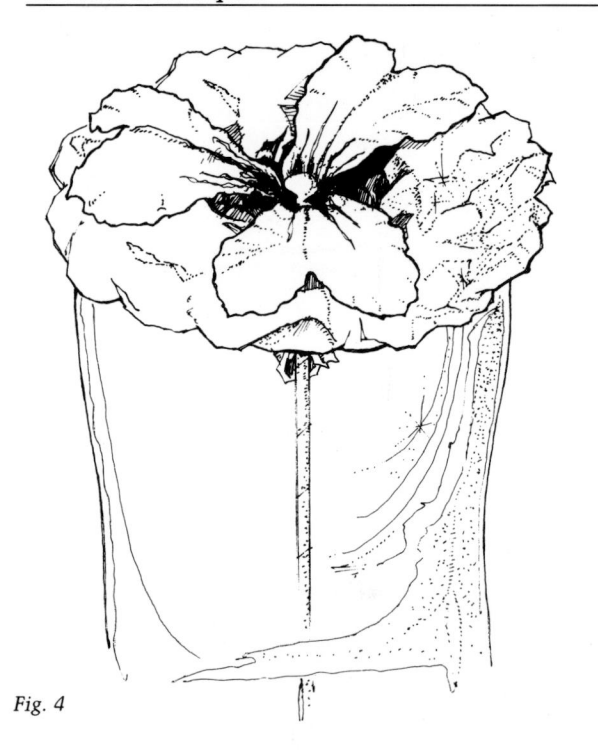

attached. Let dry overnight in a flower former or a tin foil cone to shape like a triangle. *See figure 4.*

Roll out gum-paste, very thinly, and cut out 3 large petals. Ruffle around the wide part of the petal with the pewter tool. *See figure 5*. Vein the petals, fold in half lengthwise to give a crease effect, and with the dried petals being held upside down, attach the lower petals with gum glue approximately 1/4" (5mm) from the bottom of the dried petals. *See figure 6*. Fold the larger petal back and at the same time hollow out the two petals. *See figure 7*. Let dry upside down overnight. Roll out gum-paste, very thinly, and cut out 3 thin petals. *See figure 8*. Ruffle around the top half of the petals with the pewter tool and vein the petals. Paint the base of the thin

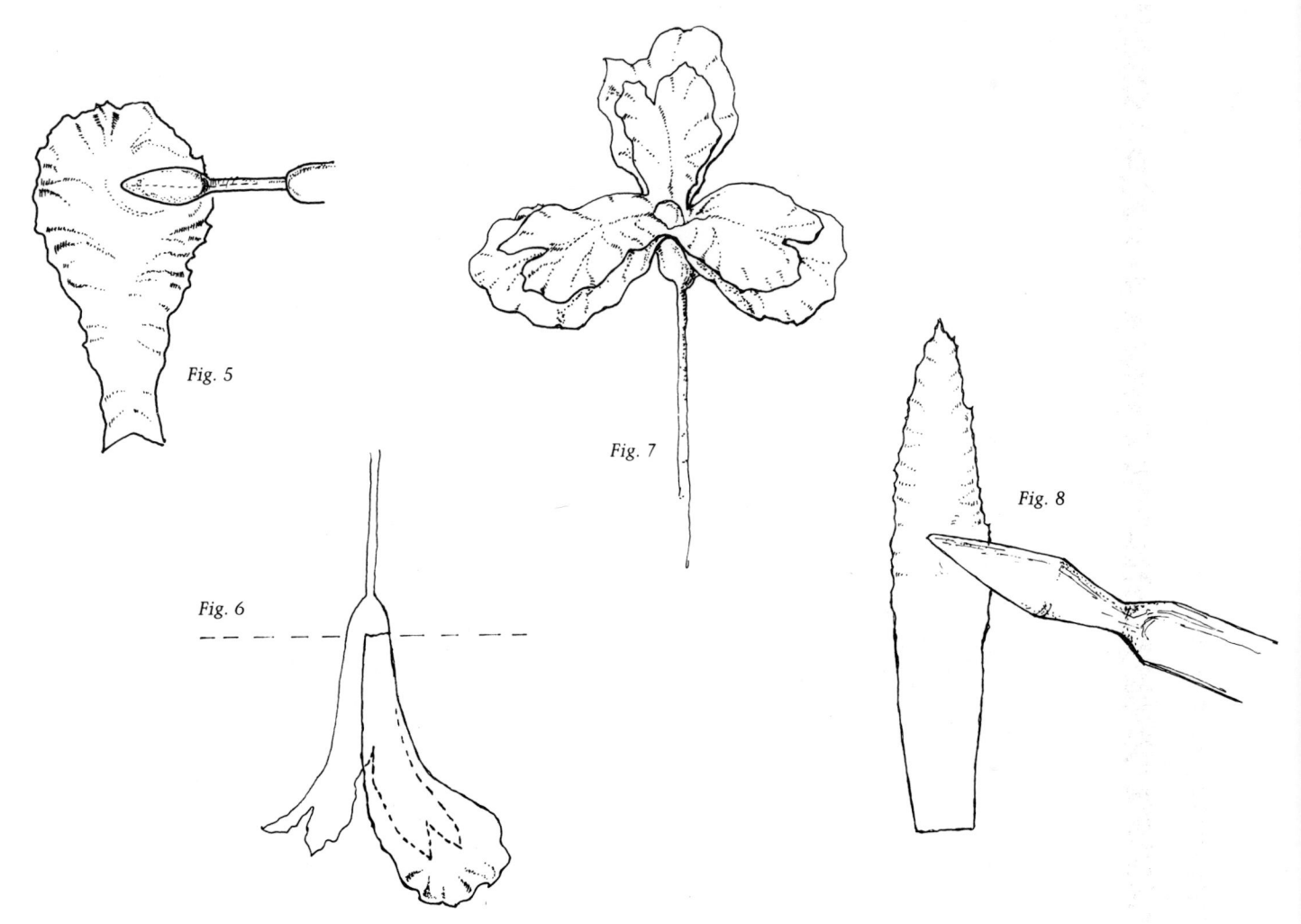

*Fig. 4*

*Fig. 5*

*Fig. 6*

*Fig. 7*

*Fig. 8*

petals with gum glue, and attach the 3 thin petals in between the other sets of petals. *See figure 9*. Let dry overnight upside down.

When dry, paint the centre of the middle large petal (the petal which was turned back) with a slight coating of water, *see figure 10*, and sprinkle either yellow coloured sugar or yellow sugartex over the water. *See figure 11*. Let dry. (If you make a blue iris, you will have to paint white, short lines around the base of the yellow sugartex).

To make the green sheath, colour some gum paste moss green and roll out gum paste very thin. Cut out two thin petals for each flower. Thin around the edges with a ball tool, vein the sheath, paint the inside of the sheath with gum glue and attach one sheath to either side of the flower. *See figure 12*. Let dry overnight.

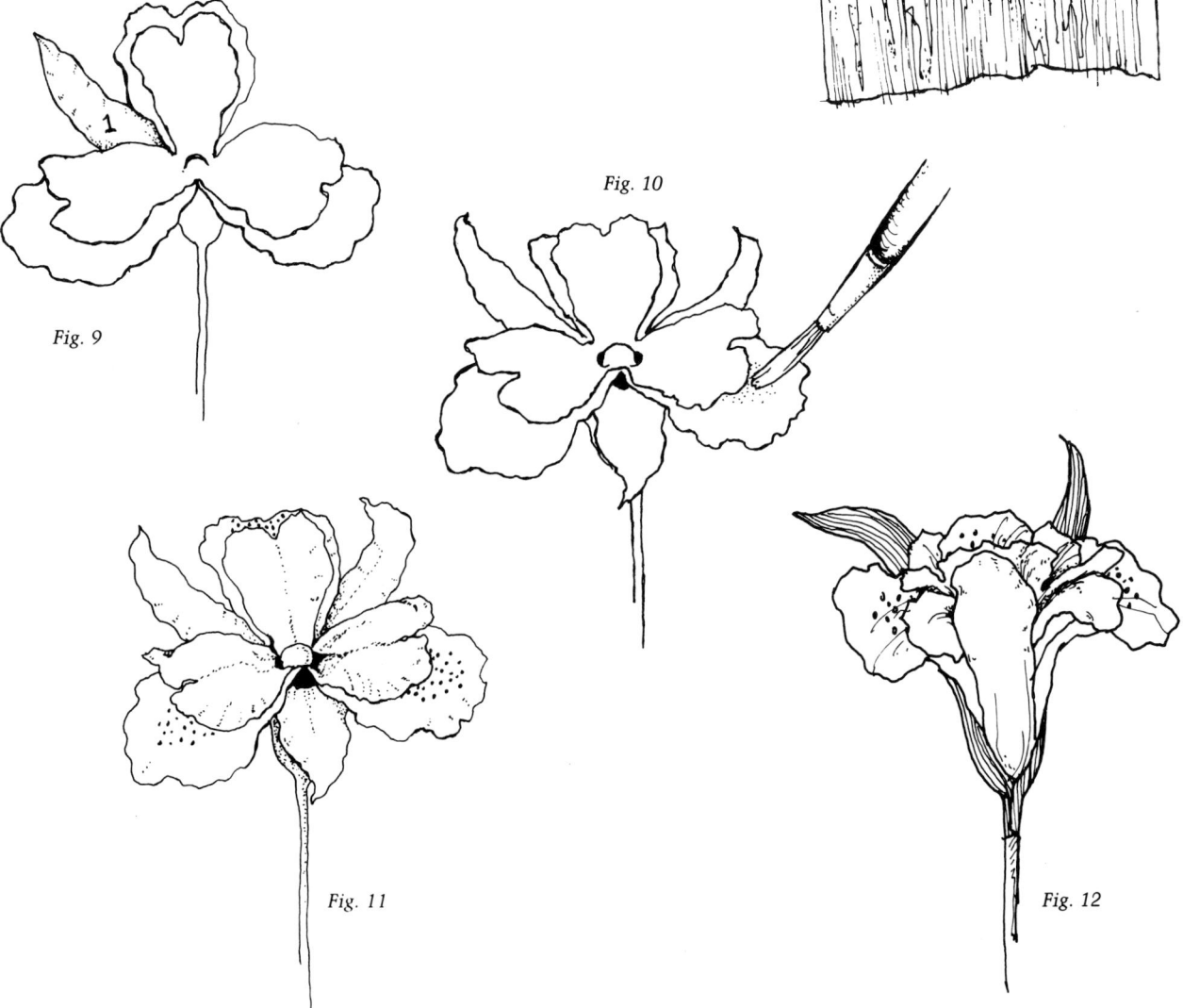

Fig. 8

Fig. 9

Fig. 10

Fig. 11

Fig. 12

Fig. 1

False Collar

Fig. 2

Fig. 3

Fig. 4

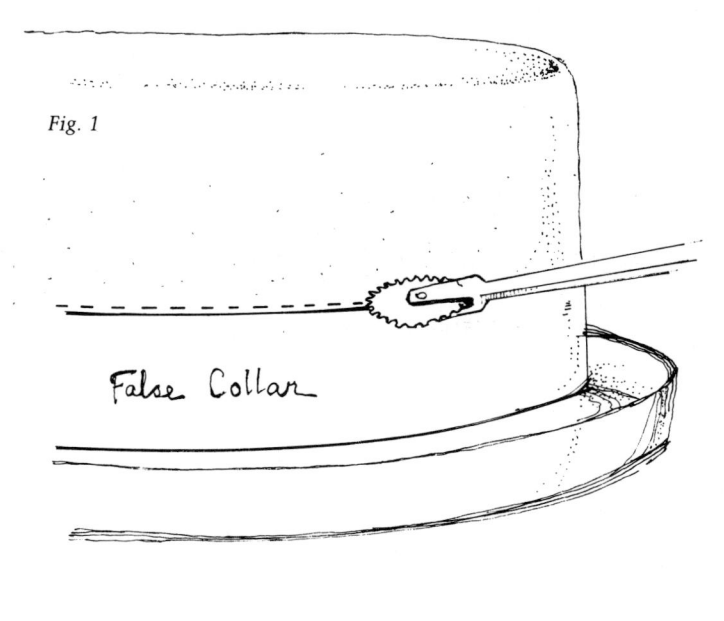

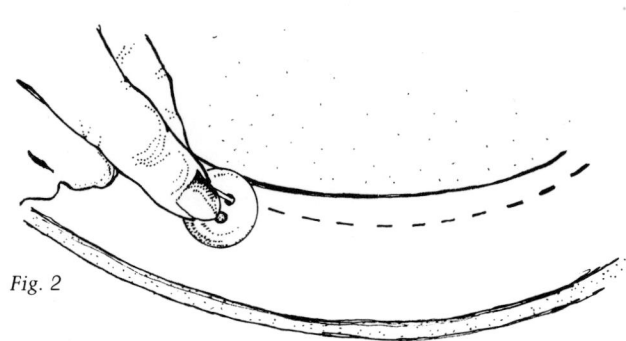

## Cross-Over Cake

A striking and effective new design:

*Step 1:* Cover the board with fondant following instructions on page 10, and let dry overnight. Cover the cake with fondant and place on the board. With a #2 tip, pipe a small bead border around the base of the cake. Let dry.

*Step 2:* Make a false collar and mark the height of the pattern on the side of the cake with a dressmaker's wheel. *See figure 1.* With a button and a toothpick inserted through the centre, move the button around the base of the cake marking a circle on the board. *See figure 2.*

*Step 3:* With a #2 tip, pipe around the marked line on the board. *See figure 3.* With a 0 tip, pipe 6 strings at an angle. Pipe 6 strings in the opposite direction, only this time, the first string must touch the first of the opposite strings. *See figure 4.* Continue this pattern all around the cake. Let dry.

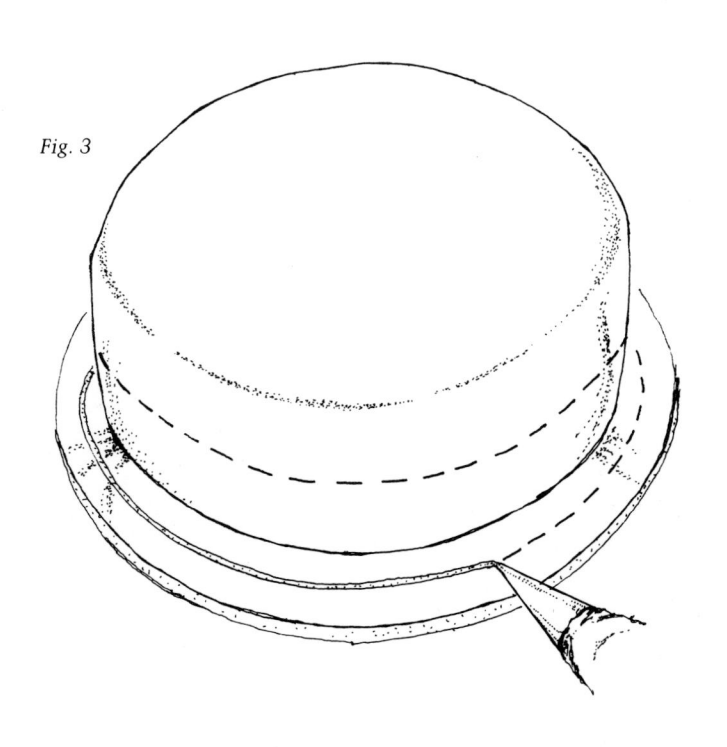

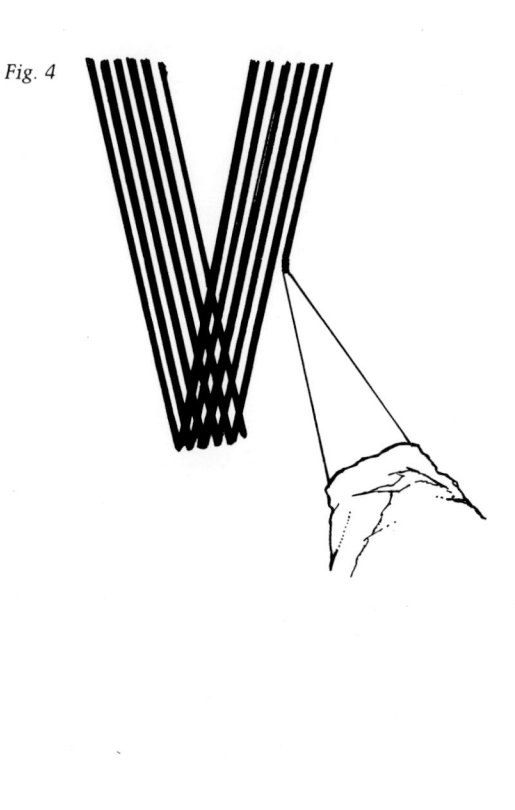

*Step 4:* Attach the ribbon around the cake making sure the ribbon fits tightly just above the top of the ends of the strings. *See figure 5.*

*Step 5:* Mark and outline the embroidery.

Make up royal icing to a count of 8 and with a #1 tip, pipe the icing into the blossoms on the side of the cake. Complete the rest of the embroidery pattern with a 0 tip. Let dry.

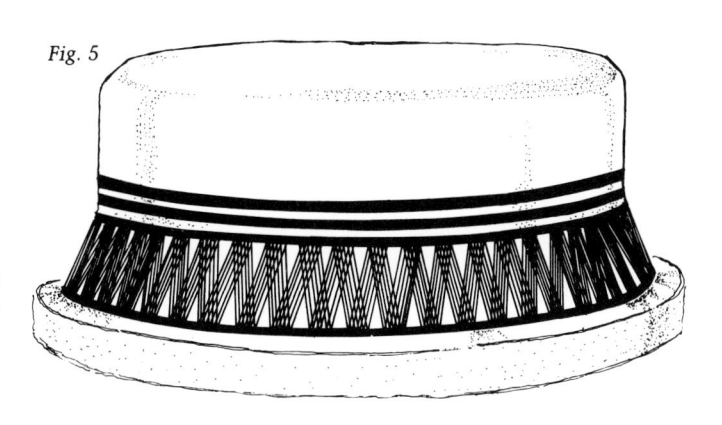

Fig. 5

# Hibiscus

Place of origin: China, introduced into Europe in 1731.

Colours: Bright pinks and reds.

Required: hibiscus cutters, crimson gum-paste, 22g covered wire, 5 red stamens, 20 small yellow headed stamens, and red dusting powder.

*Step 1:* Make a small hook on the end of the wire. Make a small roll of crimson gum-paste 1½" (38mm) and attach to the hooked wire. *See figure 1.*

*Step 2:* Tape 5 red stamens together, *see figure 2,* and attach into the end of the roll. *See figure 3.*

*Step 3:* Cut the yellow stamens to ¼" (7mm) in length, and place at random around the roll. *See figure 4.* (Do not cover more than 1" (25mm) in length). Let dry.

*Step 4:* Roll out the crimson gum-paste very thinly, and cut out 5 petals. Dust each petal from the centre down to the base of the petals. *See figure 5.* Thin around the edges of the petals with a ball tool. *See figure 6.* Vein each petal.

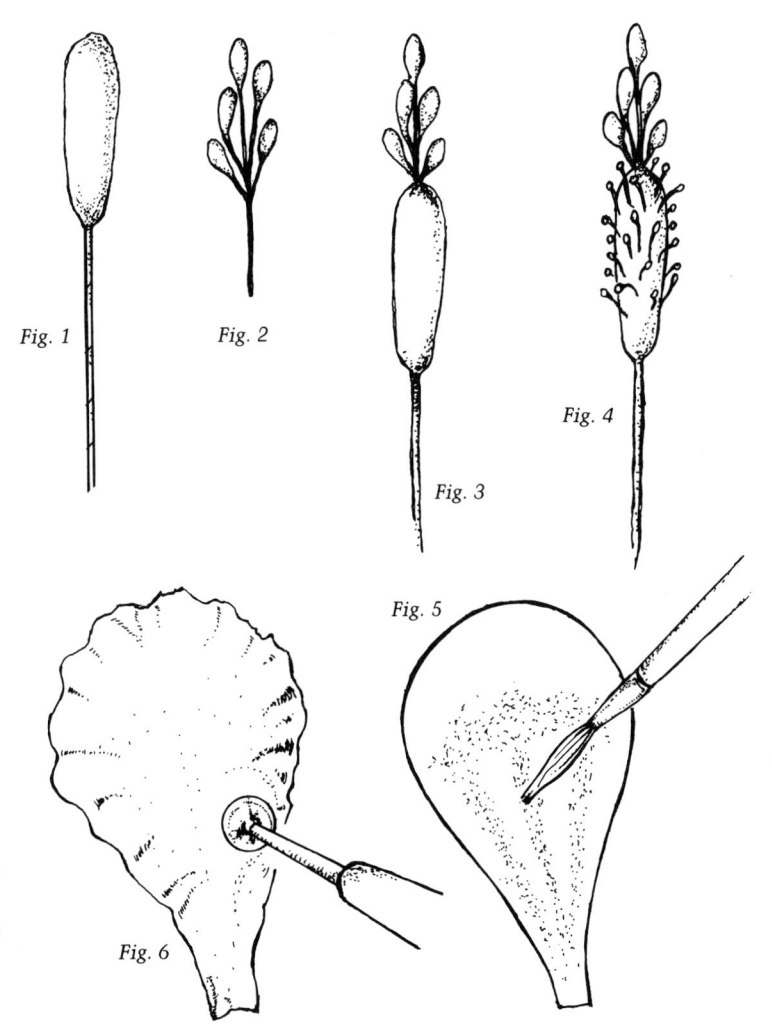

Fig. 1  Fig. 2  Fig. 3  Fig. 4  Fig. 5  Fig. 6

52  *New Techniques*

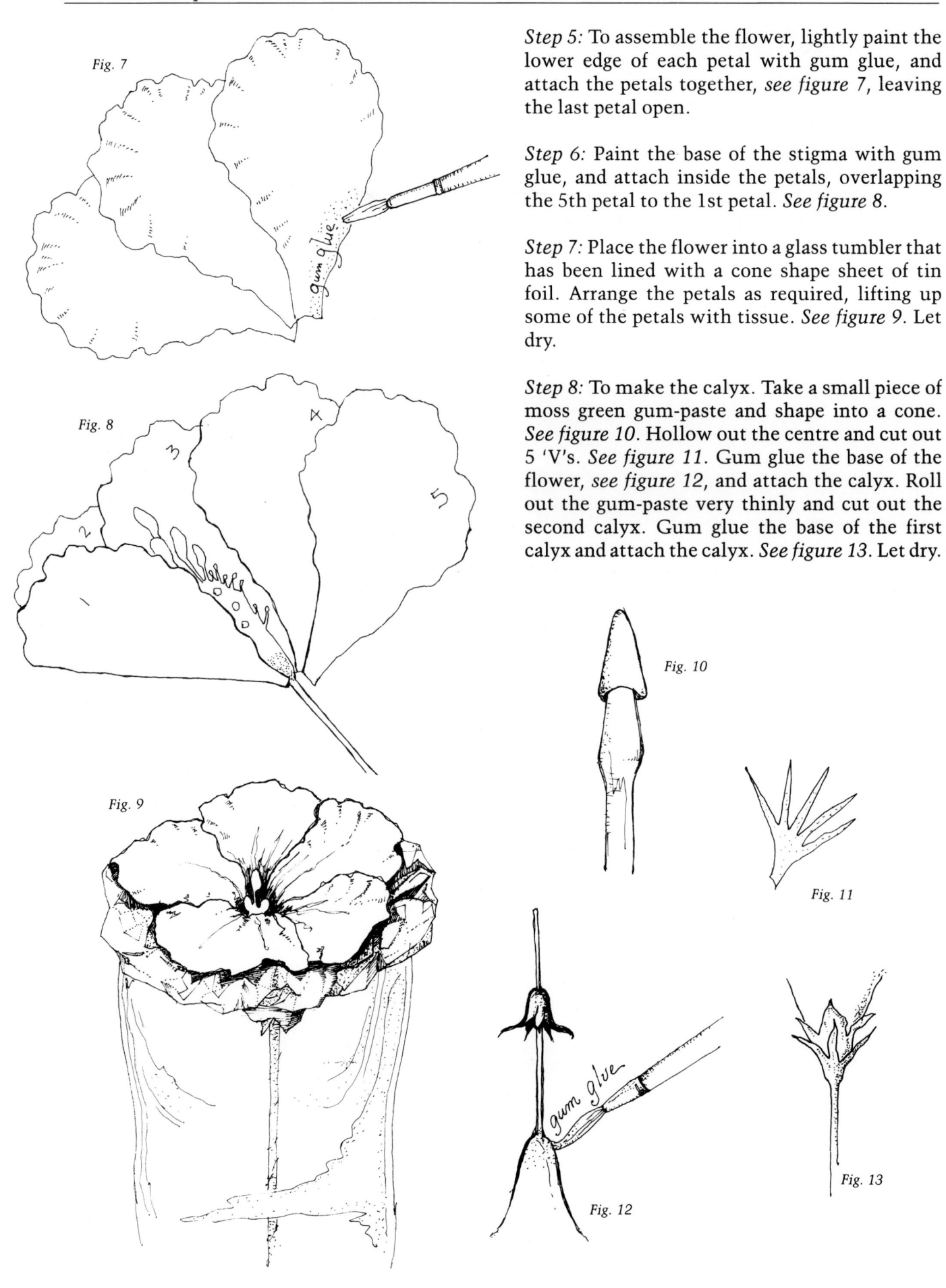

*Fig. 7*

*Fig. 8*

*Fig. 9*

*Step 5:* To assemble the flower, lightly paint the lower edge of each petal with gum glue, and attach the petals together, *see figure 7*, leaving the last petal open.

*Step 6:* Paint the base of the stigma with gum glue, and attach inside the petals, overlapping the 5th petal to the 1st petal. *See figure 8.*

*Step 7:* Place the flower into a glass tumbler that has been lined with a cone shape sheet of tin foil. Arrange the petals as required, lifting up some of the petals with tissue. *See figure 9.* Let dry.

*Step 8:* To make the calyx. Take a small piece of moss green gum-paste and shape into a cone. *See figure 10.* Hollow out the centre and cut out 5 'V's. *See figure 11.* Gum glue the base of the flower, *see figure 12*, and attach the calyx. Roll out the gum-paste very thinly and cut out the second calyx. Gum glue the base of the first calyx and attach the calyx. *See figure 13.* Let dry.

*Fig. 10*

*Fig. 11*

*Fig. 12*

*Fig. 13*

# Cymbidium Cake

Another new design without bridging which allows the darker colour to reflect through.

*Step 1:* Cover the board with fondant following instructions on page 10 and let dry overnight. Cover the cake with fondant and place on the board. With a #2 tip, pipe a small bead border around the base of the cake and let dry 2 hours.

*Step 2:* Make a false collar, this time cutting the collar into a triangular shape. *See figure 1.* Mark around the centre of the cake at the top of the triangle. Place the tip of the triangle to the desired height of the strings and the wide part of the triangle on the cake board. *See figure 2.* With a pin, mark the pattern. *See figure 3.*

*Step 3:* With a #1 tip, pipe the pattern from the cake down to the marked board, resulting in an upside down V pattern. *See figure 4.* You may have to tilt the cake towards you, or place a wedge underneath the cake board so the strings will not sag. Let dry 2 hours.

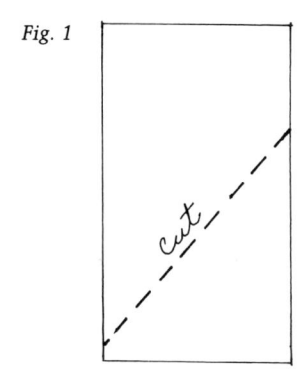

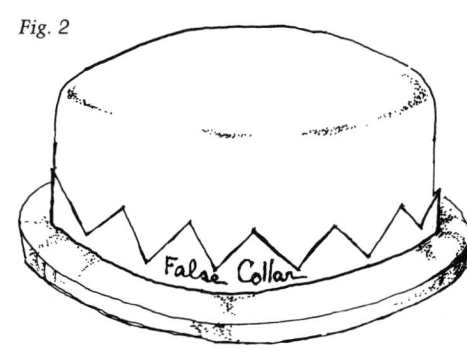

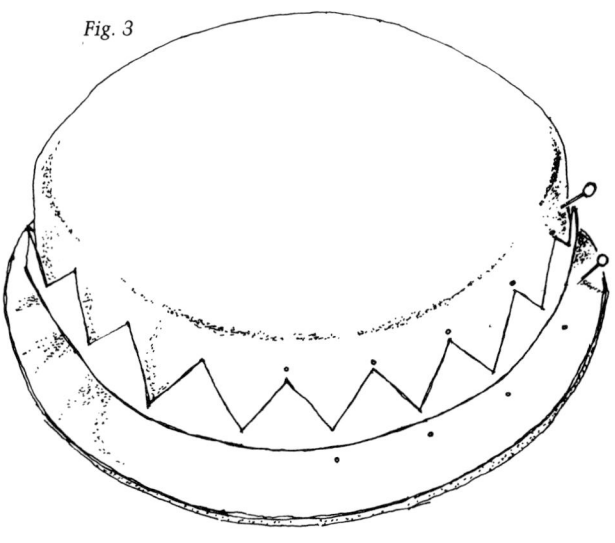

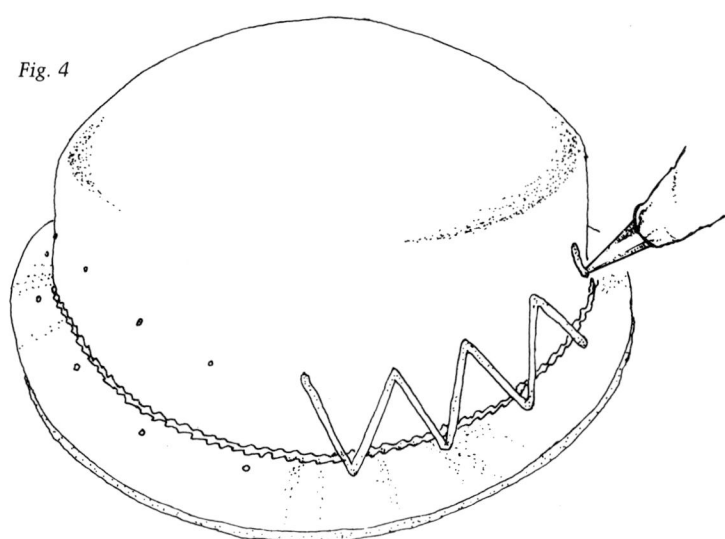

*Fig. 5*

*Fig. 6*

*Fig. 7*

*Fig. 8*

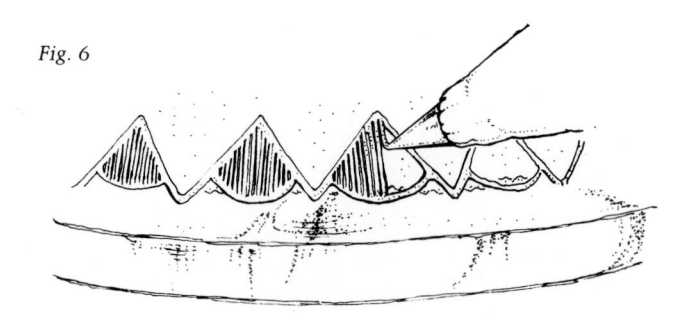

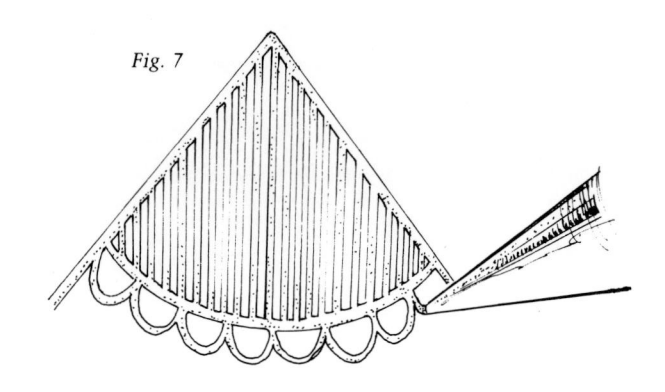

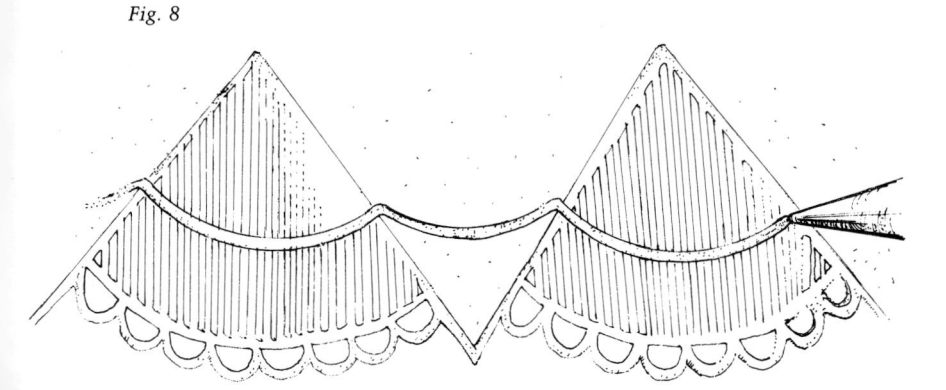

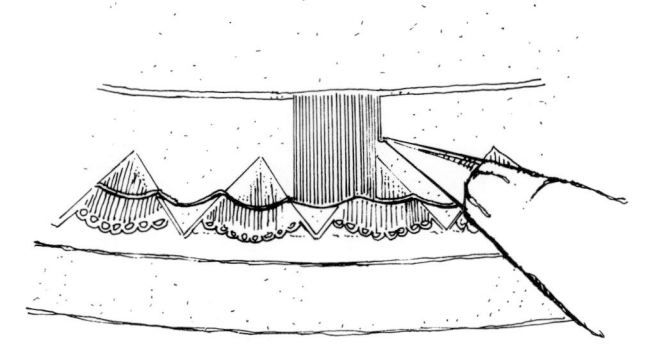

*Fig. 9*

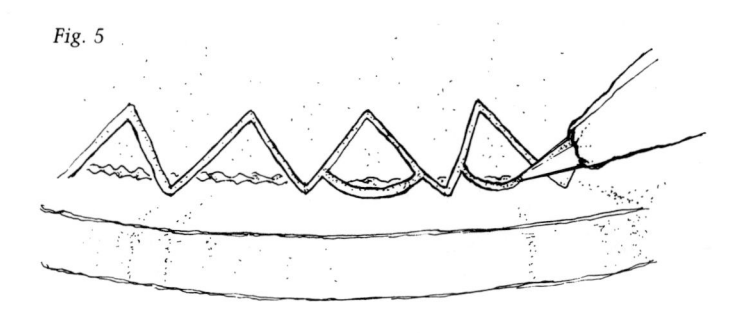

*Step 4:* With a #1 tip, pipe garlands close to the lower edge of the "V" but do not let them touch the board. *See figure 5.* Let dry 4 hours. With a 0 tip, pipe the strings in the completed triangle shape. *See figure 6.* Let dry 2 hours.

*Step 5:* Pipe the scallop at the bottom of the garland. *See figure 7.* Let dry 1 hour. With a #1 tip, pipe scallops half way down the strings. *See figure 8.* Let dry. With a 0 tip, pipe the strings from the top mark on the side of the cake to the scallop. *See figure 9.* Let dry. With a 0 tip, pipe the small scallops around the edge of the strings. *See figure 10 and 11*. Let dry. With a 0 tip, pipe a small scallop around the top of the strings and finish off by piping a small dot on each string. *See figure 12*. Let dry.

*Step 6:* Place 2 rows of ribbon around the top of the strings attaching the ribbons with a small amount of royal icing. For the embroidery pattern, pipe with a 0 tip, a cluster of three small dots at random over the cake. *See figure 13*. Let dry.

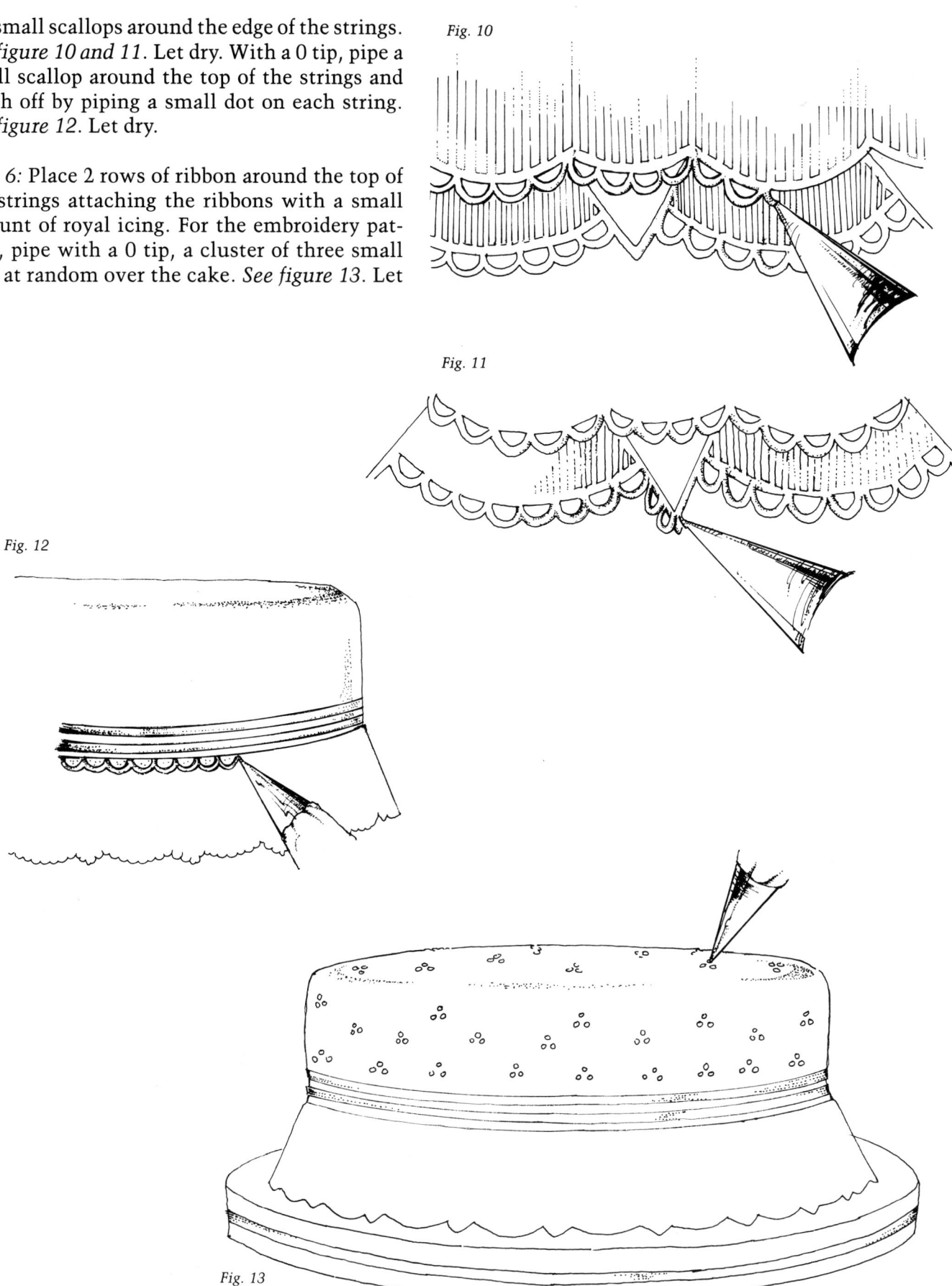

*Fig. 10*

*Fig. 11*

*Fig. 12*

*Fig. 13*

56 New Techniques

Fig. 1

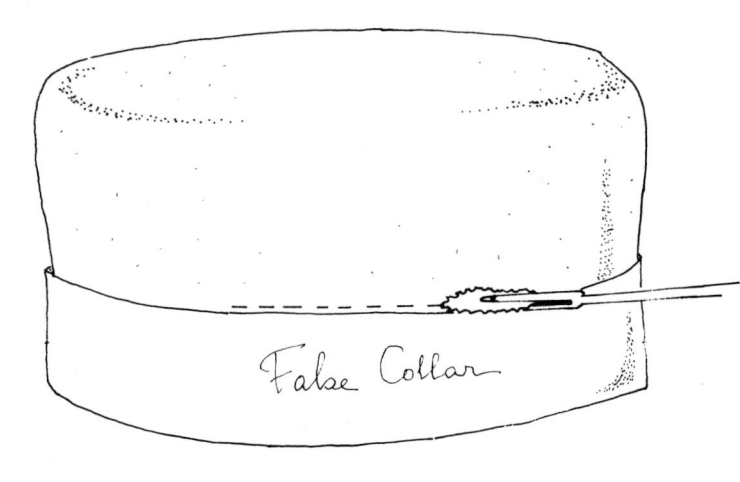

*False Collar*

Fig. 2

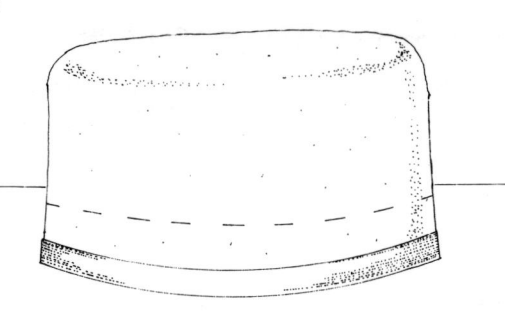

Fig. 3

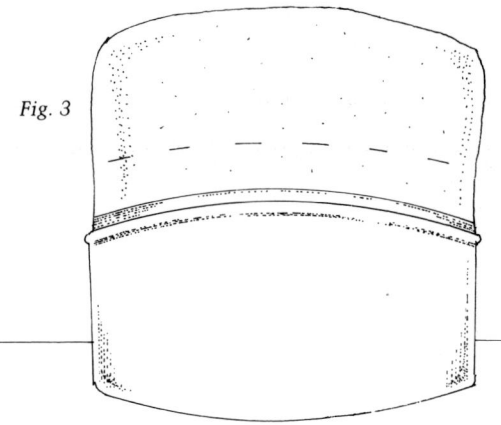

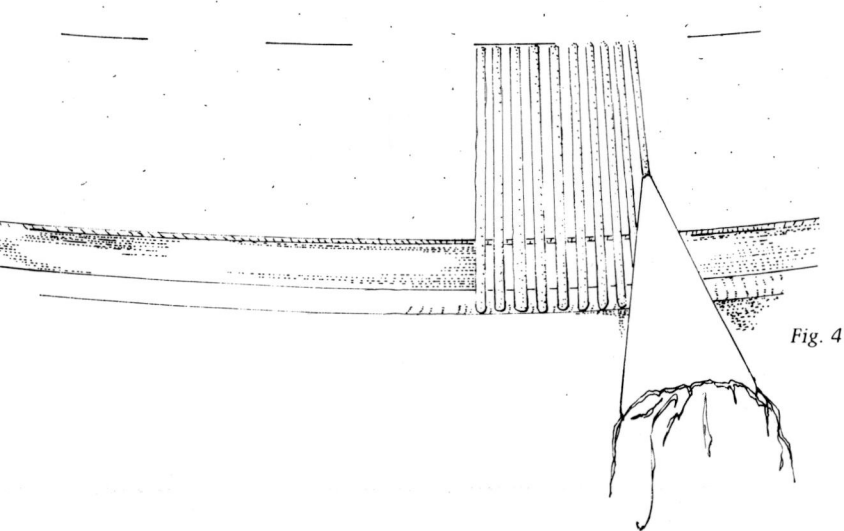

Fig. 4

# No Bridge Stringwork Cake

A completely new idea. This style of cake requires two cake boards. One board the exact size of the cake which must be covered attached to the cake. The other cake board will be covered and used to stand the cake on.

*Step 1:* Cover the board with fondant following instructions on page 10, and let dry overnight. Cover the cake and board with fondant. Let dry.

*Step 2:* Make a false collar, this time mark the centre of the sides of the cake. *See figure 1*. Attach the ribbon around the base of the cake with royal icing. *See figure 2*. If you make a 6" (15 cm) cake, take an empty 8" (20.3 cm) cake tin and lightly grease the top edge of the tin to help release the strings when dry. Place a 4" dummy cake into the cake tin, then place the fondant cake on top of the dummy. (The cake should be slightly below the edge of the top of the cake tin. *See figure 3*.) With a 0 tip, pipe the strings from the top pattern line to the top edge of the cake tin. *See figure 4*. This cake *cannot* be

BLUE CAKE—DOUBLE STRING WORK

57

ANNIVERSARY CAKE

CROSS-OVER CAKE

**NO BRIDGE STRINGWORK CAKE**

removed until the entire cake has been decorated and well dried. With a 0 tip, pipe small scallops all around the cake and continue until you reach the base of the strings. *See figure 5.* Let dry. Pipe a small bead border around the top strings with a 0 tip. Let dry 2 hours. *See figure 6.*

*Step 3:* Take the covered cake board and place a small amount of icing in the centre of the board. Carefully remove the cake from the tin and place on the board.

*Step 4:* Apply the cameo with royal icing. Mark and pipe embroidery with a 0 tip and let dry. *(See page 15 for instructions on filet crochet.)*

Fig. 5

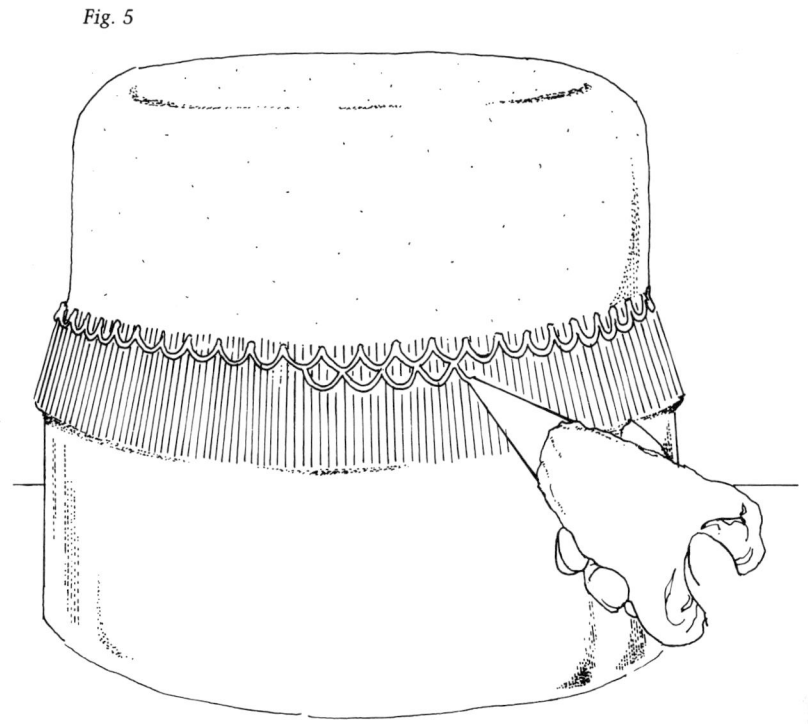

Fig. 6

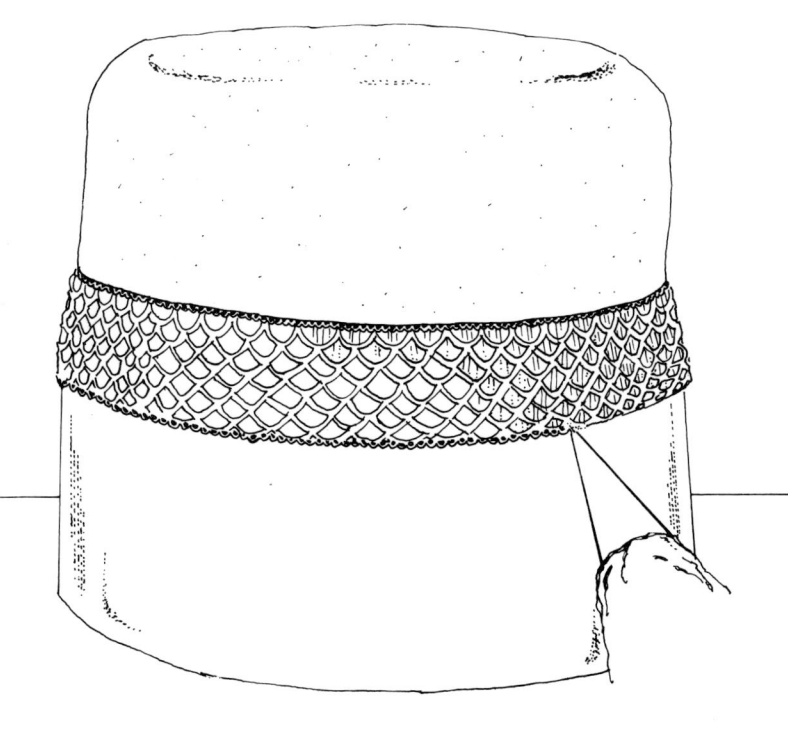

## Two-Tier White Cake

A new design for bridging which makes the cake very elegant!

*Step 1:* Cover the board with fondant following instructions on page 10, and let dry overnight. Cover the cake with fondant and place on the board. With a #2 tip, pipe a small bead border around the base of the cakes and let dry *2 days*.

*Step 2:* Make a false collar and attach to the cake. Mark the top edge of the collar on the sides of the cake with a dressmaker's wheel. For the bridging on the boards, use a button with a toothpick inserted through the centre and run the button around the base of the cake making sure to mark a fine outline. *See figure 1.* (This determines and marks a consistent measurement from the base of the cake to the outermost perimeter of the scallops). Measure the perimeter and divide into equal parts no greater than 1½" (3.8 cm). Using a divider with the tips parted to the required distance mark the boards to prepare for the scallops. *See figure 2.*

*Step 3:* Turn both the board and cake upside-down on to a smaller 6" (15 mm) styro dummy cake to elevate. With a #2 tip, pipe scallops from mark to mark. *See figure 3.* Let dry 4–6 hours or

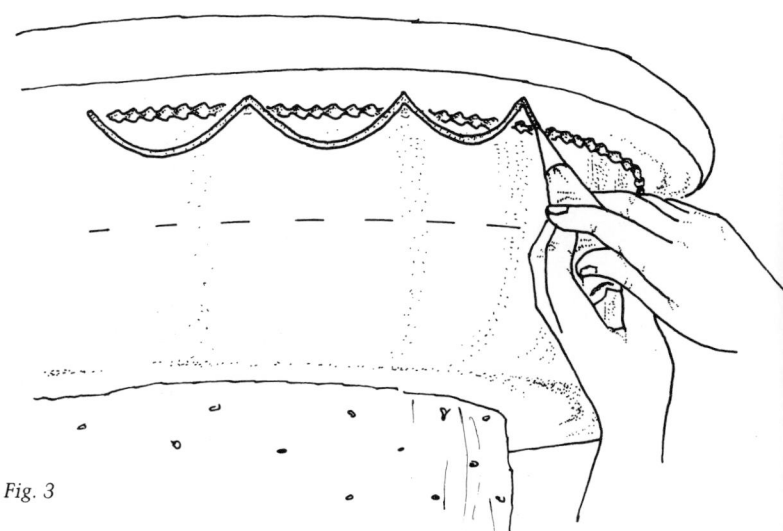

*Fig. 1*

*Fig. 2*

*Fig. 3*

overnight. Turn the cake right side up and with a 0 tip pipe strings from the previous marked line on the side of the cake down to the scallop, taking care not to put too much pressure on the scallop or it will break. *See figure 4.* Let dry 2 hours or overnight.

*Step 4:* Pipe a small scallop around the top of the strings to finish and make the top of the strings look neat. *See figure 5.* Pipe small "C" upside-down at the top edge of the strings. *See figure 6.* Let dry. With a 0 tip pipe small scallops around the scallop bridge. *See figure 7.*

*Step 5:* Attach two rows of ribbon around the cake just above the line of piped "c's" and secure the ribbons with a small amount of royal icing. *See figure 8.* Mark and pipe the embroidery with a 0 tip and let dry. Repeat for top tier.

*Fig. 4*

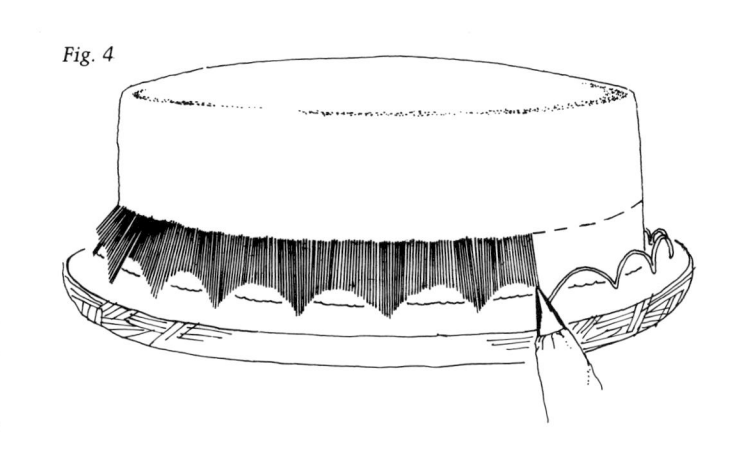

*Fig. 5*

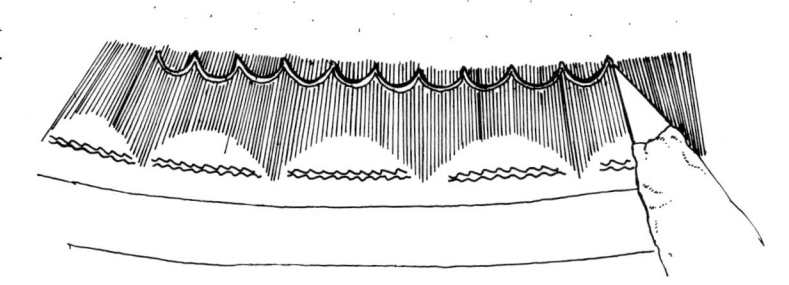

*Fig. 6*

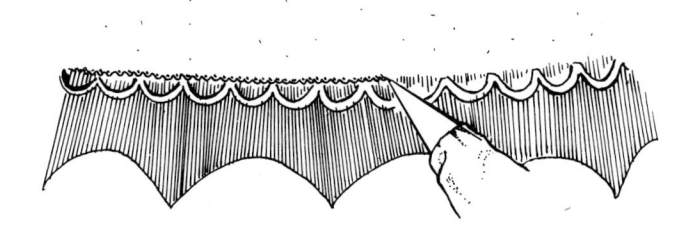

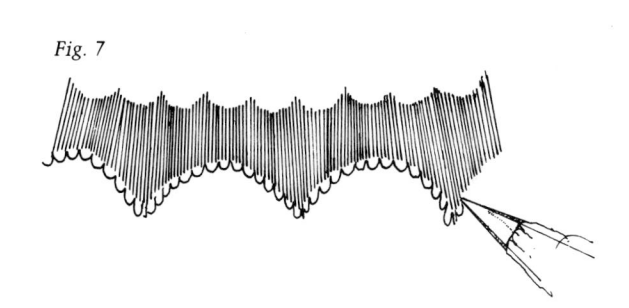

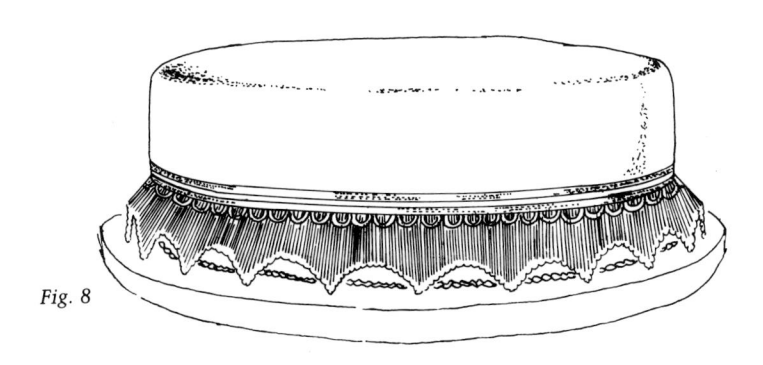

*Fig. 7*

*Fig. 8*

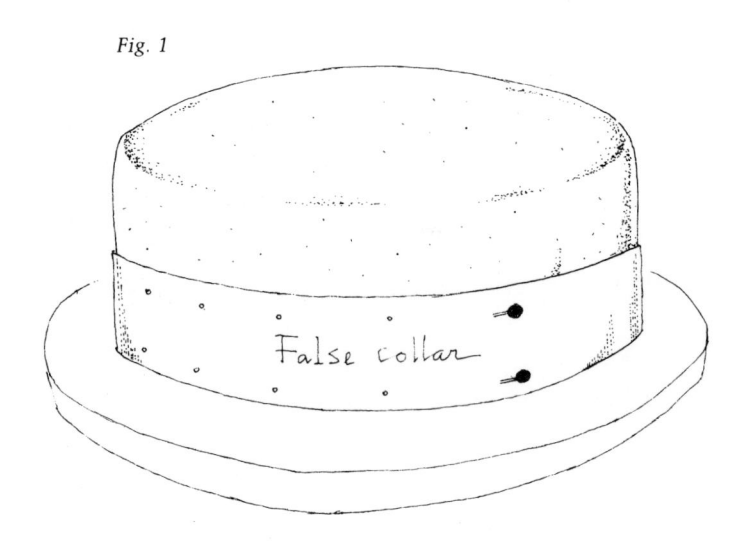

# White & Burgundy Cake

This cake with the upper and lower scallop bridge gives a most striking effect.

*Step 1:* Cover the board with fondant following instructions on page 10, and let dry overnight. Cover the cake with fondant and place on the board. With a #2 tip pipe a small bead border around the base of the cake. Let the cake dry for at least 2 days.

*Step 2:* Make a false collar and mark the pattern at both the top and base on the sides of the cake. Attach the ribbon just above the small bead border. *See figure 1.*

*Step 3:* With a #1 tip and royal icing, pipe small dots on the marked pattern. Let dry.

*Step 4:* Place a small round cake board on top of the cake, and very gently tip and press the large cake board to the wall. *See figure 2.*

*Step 5:* With a 0 tip pipe scallops first at the top marked line, then at the lower marked line. Pipe each pair of scallops before very gently turning the cake around, keeping the cake pressed against the wall, and at the same time allowing each scallop to dry before piping a second scallop. (You must take care that you do NOT pipe the top scallop larger than the lower scallop). Let dry.

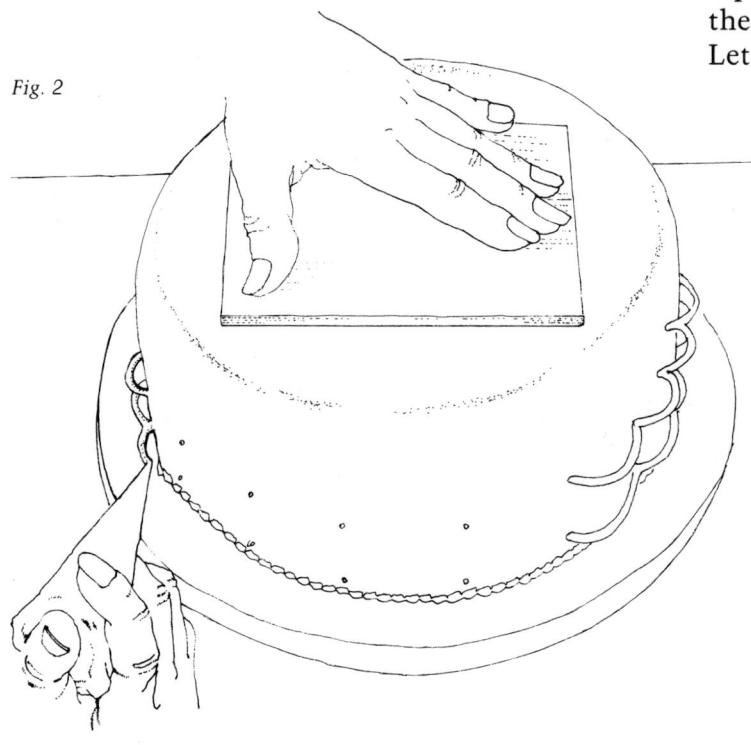

Fig. 1

Fig. 2

*Step 6:* With a 0 tip pipe strings from the top scallop to the lower scallop. Let dry. *See figure 3.* (Do not put any pressure on the scallop bridge or else they will break).

*Step 7:* With a 0 tip pipe small scallops around the lower edge of strings. Let dry. *See figure 4.*

*Step 8:* Turn the cake up-side-down and place the cake onto a tin, and with a 0 tip pipe scallops at the lower edge of strings. Let dry. *See figure 5.*

*Step 9:* Pipe the small embroidery pieces on a sheet of wax paper, let dry, then very carefully attach the embroidery pieces to the cake. Let dry.

Fig. 3

Fig. 4

Fig. 5

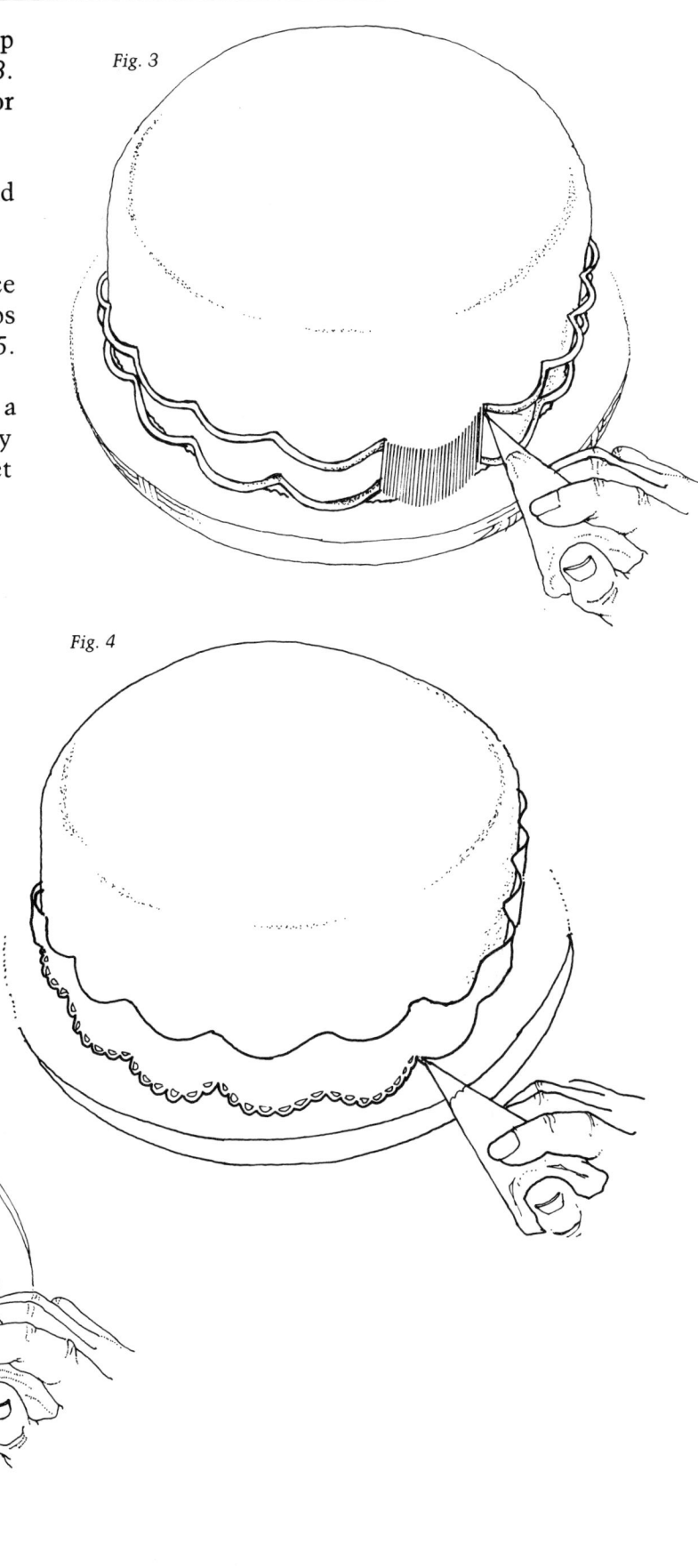

# Floating Collars

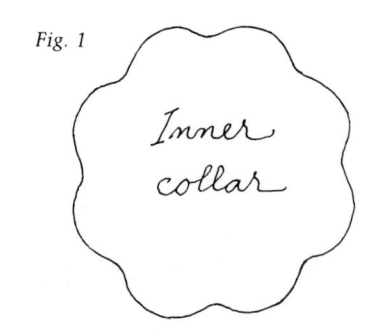

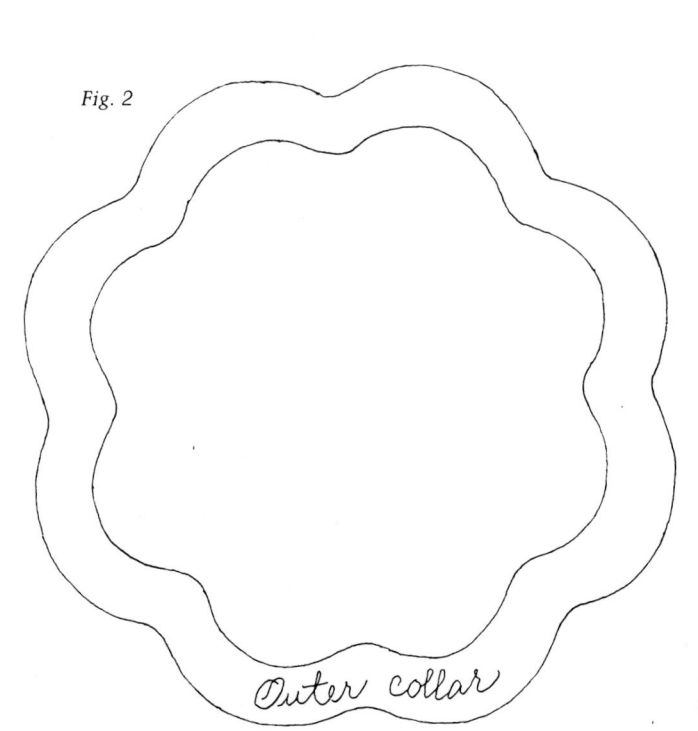

*Fig. 1* — Inner collar

*Fig. 2* — Outer collar

*Fig. 3*

## Beige Double Collar Cake, 1983

This cake was originally made for display at the 1983 INTERNATIONAL CAKE EXPLORATION SOCIETY.

*Step 1:* Cover the board with fondant following instructions on page 10, and let dry overnight. Cover the cake with fondant and place on the board. With a #2 tip, pipe a small bead border around the base of the cake and let dry. Cut out two gum-paste plaques for the inner collar and let dry. *See figure 1.* Roll out gum-paste and cut out the larger outer collar and let dry. *See figure 2.*

*Step 2:* Make a false collar and attach it to the cake. With a dressmaker's wheel, mark the sides of the cake. Mark the lower scallops with a pin. *See figure 3.*

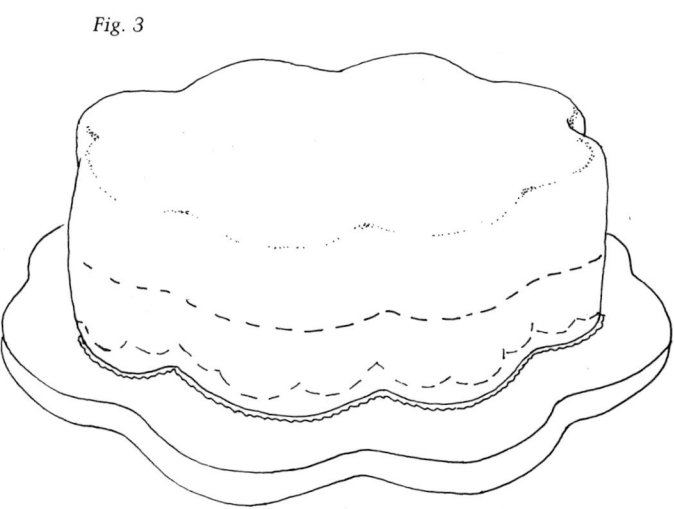

*Step 3:* With a #2 tip, pipe the bridging on the cake and let dry. With royal icing to the count of 10, flood-in the bridging and let dry.

*Step 4:* With a 0 or #1 tip, pipe the strings from the top marked line to the bridge and let dry. *See figure 4.*

*Step 5:* Make up approximately 500 lace pieces and let dry.

*Step 6:* Attach the ribbon around the cake. *See figure 5.*

*Step 7:* Take the smaller gum-paste collars and with a wooden support pipe the lines first one quarter way around the collar, then pipe the opposite string work. *See figure 6.* Let dry. Very carefully remove the supports and finish piping the strings around the circle.

*Step 8:* Place the larger collar on the cake and mark the collar around the cake, inside and outside the collar. Remove the collar and pipe a small bead border around the markings with a #1 tip. *See figure 7.* Let dry. Place the collar back on the cake, this time placing the wooden blocks under the collar. With a 0 tip, pipe the

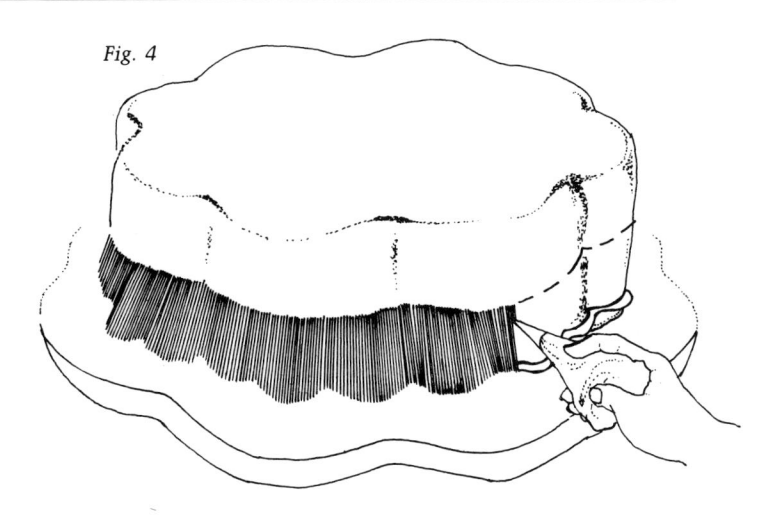

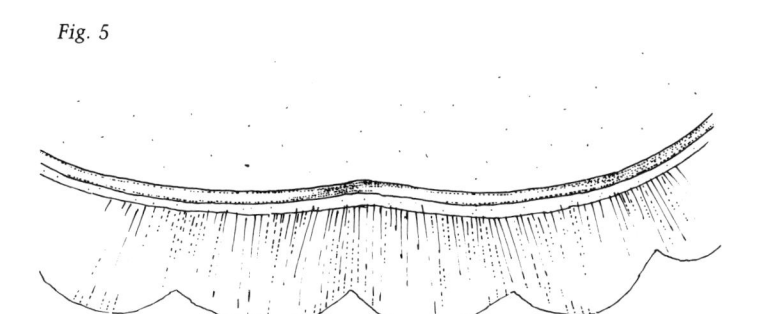

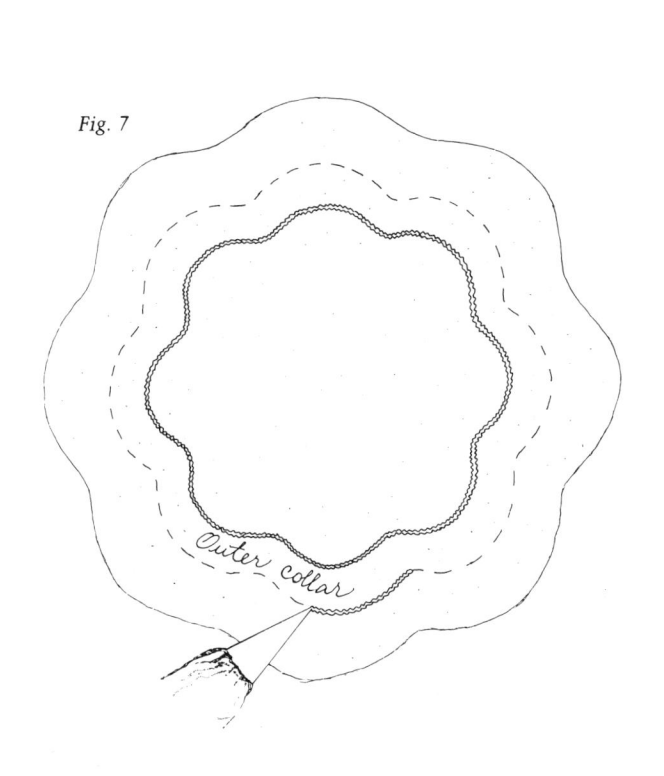

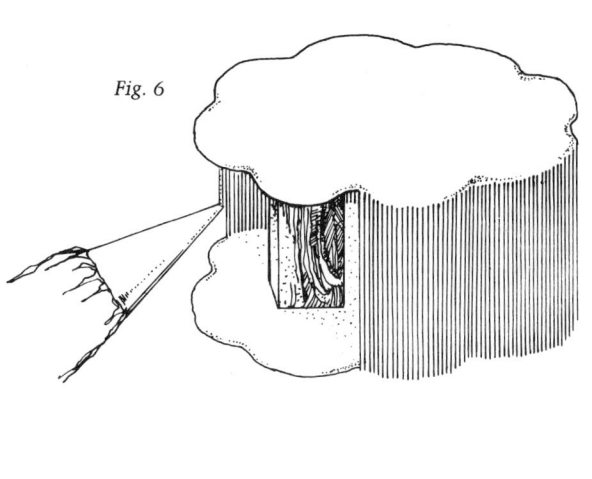

*Fig. 8*

*Fig. 9*

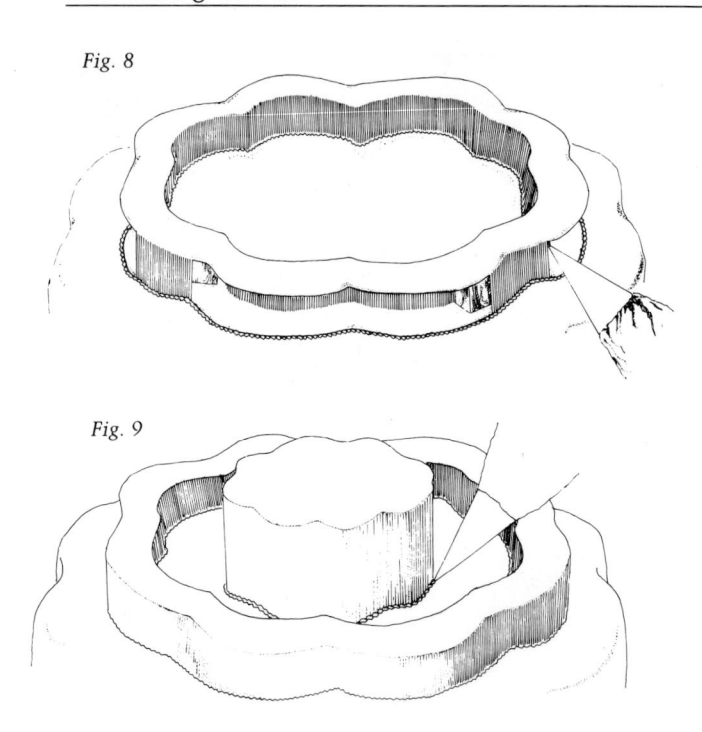

strings first inside the collar and let dry. When piping the outside of the collar, pipe the strings between the wooden blocks first. Let dry. *See figure 8*. Very gently slide the first wooden block out and pipe the strings in that area and let dry. Continue very carefully removing the wooden blocks and piping the strings where the wooden blocks were removed.

*Step 9:* To place the smaller collar into the centre of the cake, first place a small amount of royal icing in the centre of the cake. Very carefully place the collar into the centre and pipe a very small bead border around the base. *See figure 9*. With a 0 tip, pipe the strings between the small collar to the larger collar and let dry.

*Step 10:* Pipe the strings from the outer large collar to the edge of the cake. *See figure 10*.

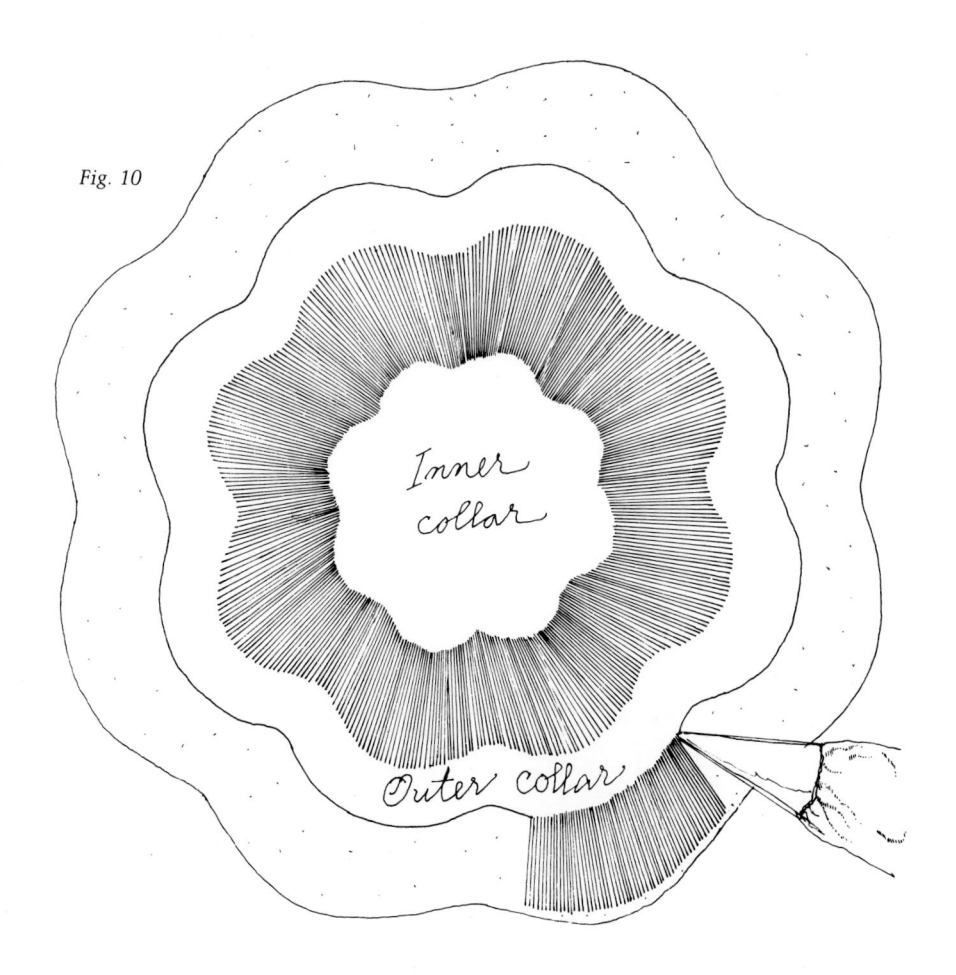

*Fig. 10*

Inner collar

Outer collar

CYMBIDIUM CAKE

TWO-TIER WHITE CAKE—*Detail*

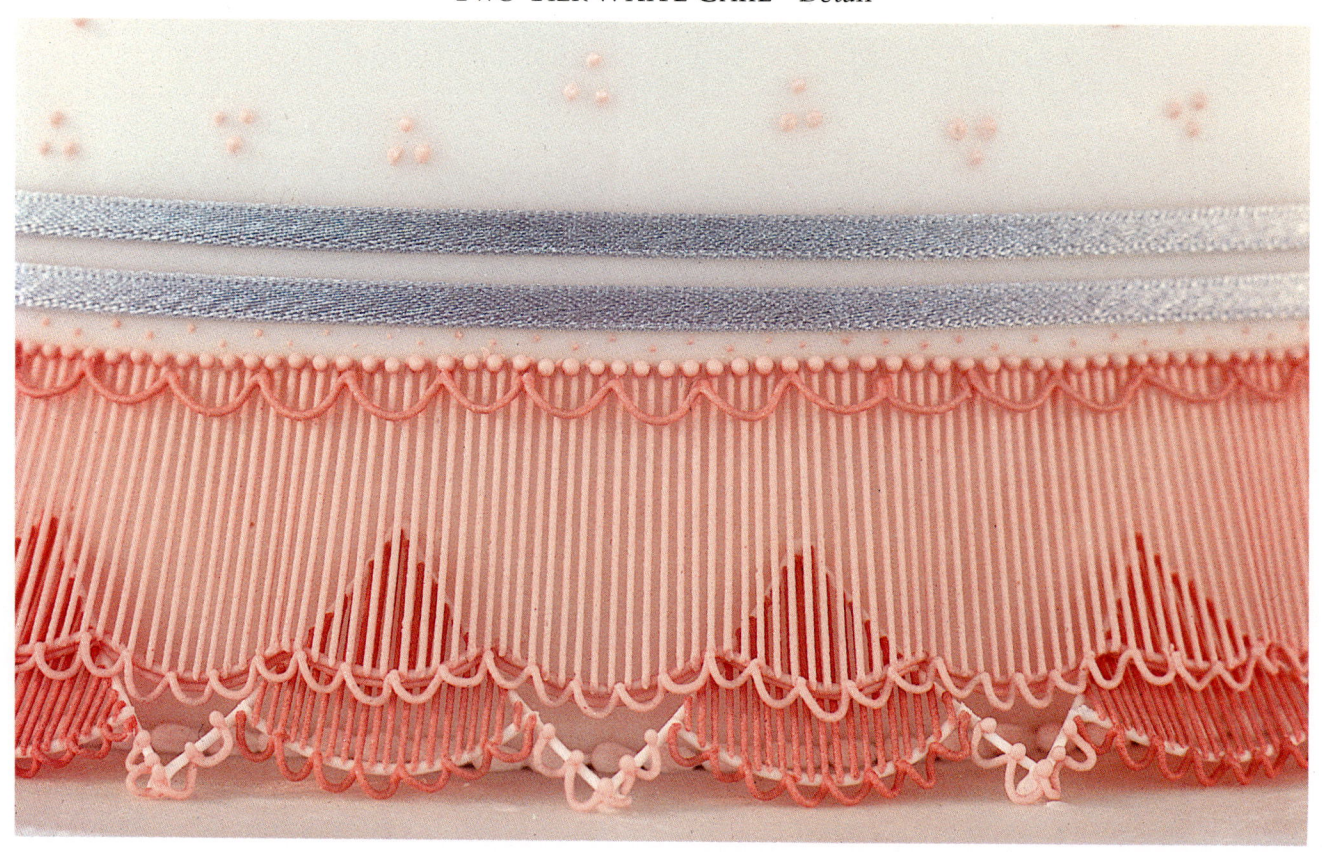

CYMBIDIUM CAKE—*Detail*

TWO-TIER WHITE CAKE

**WINNING CAKE FROM LONDON**

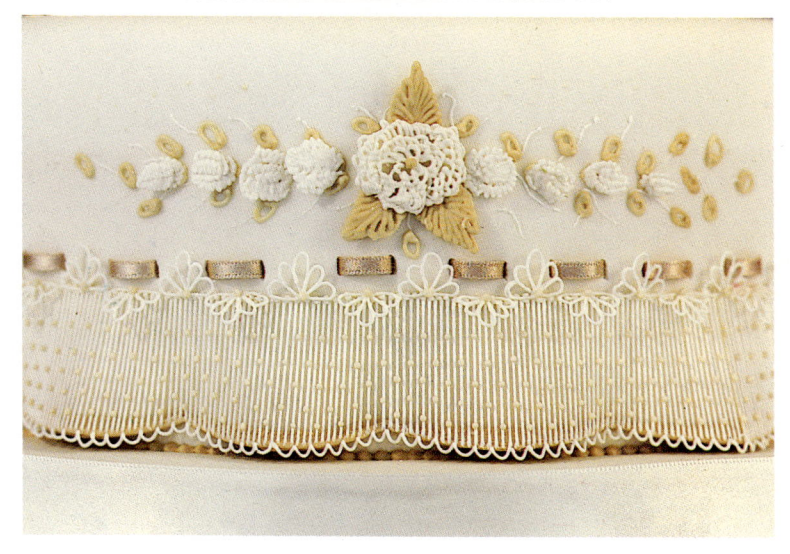

72

WHITE AND BURGUNDY CAKE

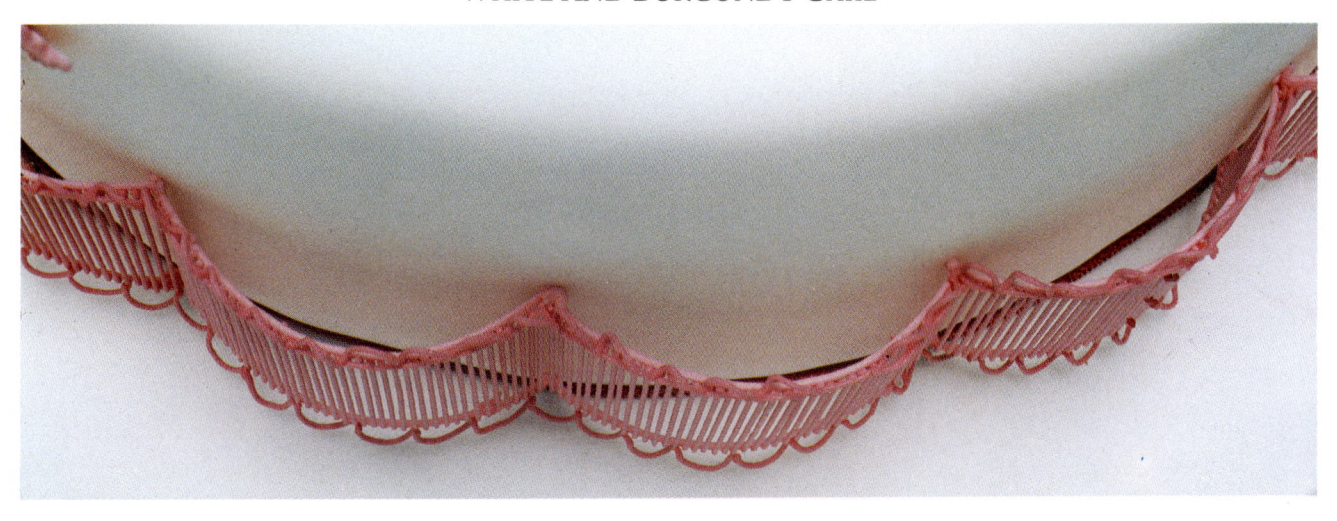

73

TWO-TIER WHITE FLOATING COLLAR CAKE

GREEN AND WHITE CAKE

TWO-TIER PINK CAKE WITH ROSES

*Step 11:* With a 0 tip attach the lace pieces to the top of the strings, and the top of the ribbon. Let dry. *See figure 11.* With a 0 tip pipe picot at the base of the strings. Let dry. *See figure 12.* Figure 13 shows the completed cake. This cake was one of the most difficult cakes to decorate.

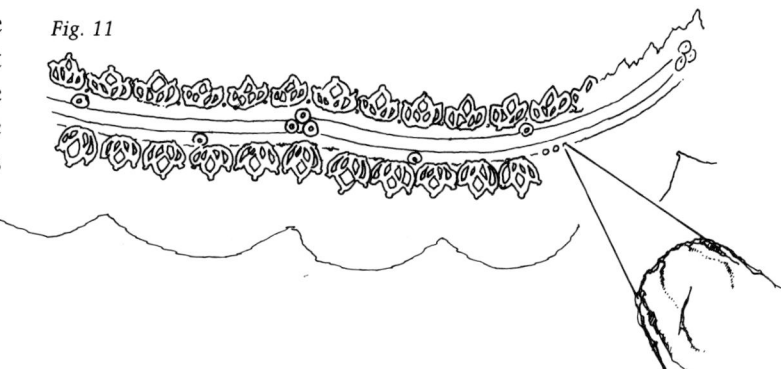

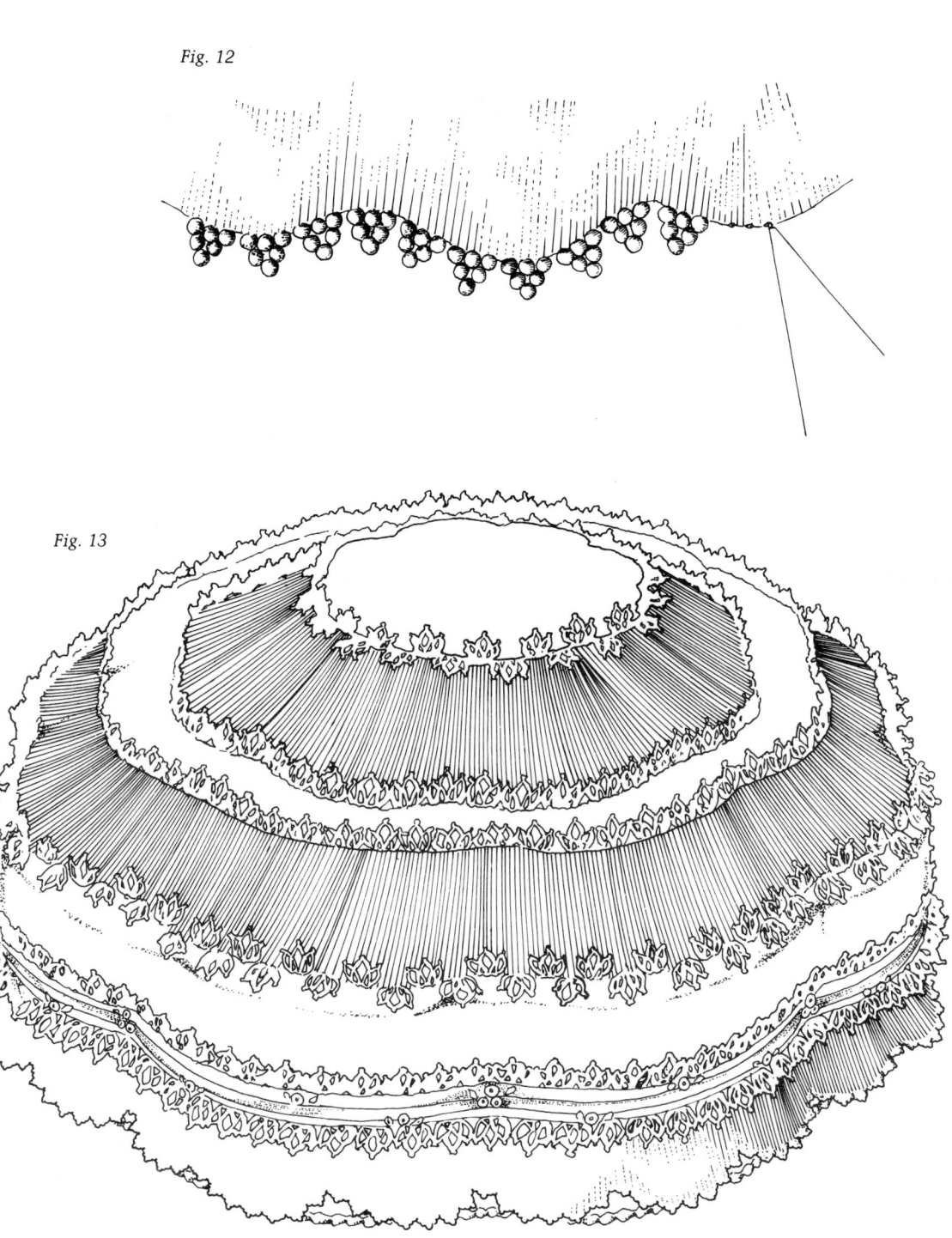

Fig. 11

Fig. 12

Fig. 13

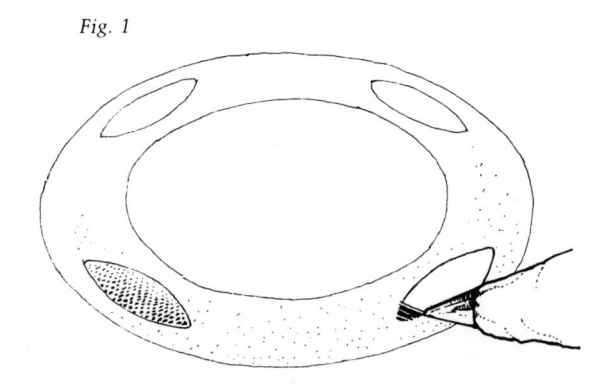

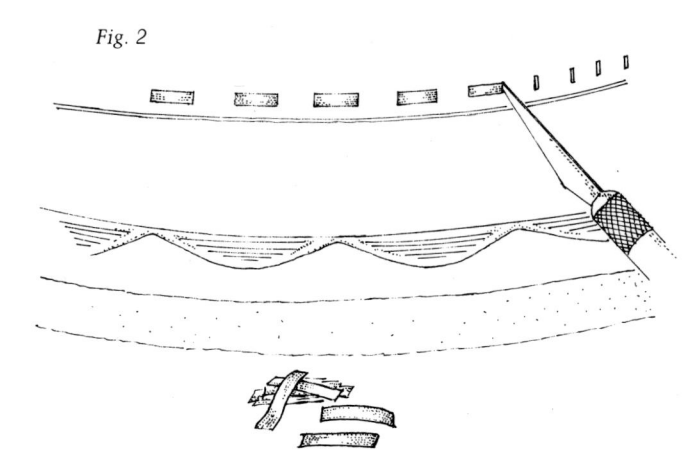

# Winning Cake from London

*Step 1:* Cover the board with fondant following instructions on page 10, and let dry overnight. Cover the cake with fondant and place on the board. With a #2 tip, pipe a bead border around the base of the cake and let dry.

*Step 2:* Make a flood-in collar (see flood-in, page 16) only this time mark a design on the top collar and with a #1 tip, outline both the inner pattern and the outer circle. *See figure 1.* Let dry 24–48 hours.

*Step 3:* Make a false collar and mark the sides of the cake. With a #2 tip, pipe the bridging on the sides of the cake and let dry. With royal icing to the count of 10, flood in the bridge and let dry while attaching the ribbon insertion. *See figure 2.*

*Step 4:* Very carefully, peel the flood-in collar from the cooking film and attach to the top of the cake, resting the collar on the wooden blocks. (1½" (3.8 cm) by 1" (2.5 cm)).

*Step 5:* With a 0 tip, or #1 tip, pipe a solid row of scallops all around the inside of the collar. *See figure 3.* Let dry.

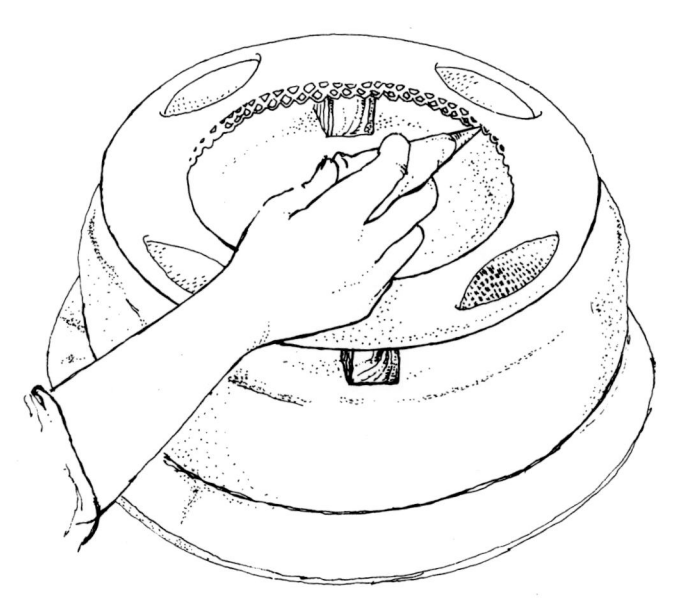

*Fig. 1*

*Fig. 2*

*Step 6:* With a 0 tip, and royal icing to the count of 8, pipe small dots on each join of the scallop and let dry. *See figure 4.*

*Step 7:* Pipe a series of scallops in between the wooden blocks on the outer collar (the scallops should be first 5, then 4 scallops, then 3, 2, 1. *See figure 5.* Let dry. With a 0 tip, repeat the dots on the outer scallops.

*Step 8:* With a 0 or #1 tip, attach the strings from the side marked line to the bridge. Let dry.

*Step 9:* Make up lace pieces and let dry. With a 0 tip, and royal icing to the count of 8, pipe dots on the strings. *See figure 6.* Attach the lace pieces, one piece going up, the other lace piece being placed looking down at an angle. *See figure 7.* Let dry.

*Step 10:* Pipe the side and top embroidery pieces. Let dry. With a 0 tip pipe royal icing on the back of the embroidery pieces, and attach to the collar and the sides of the cake. Let dry.

Fig. 5

Fig. 6

Fig. 4

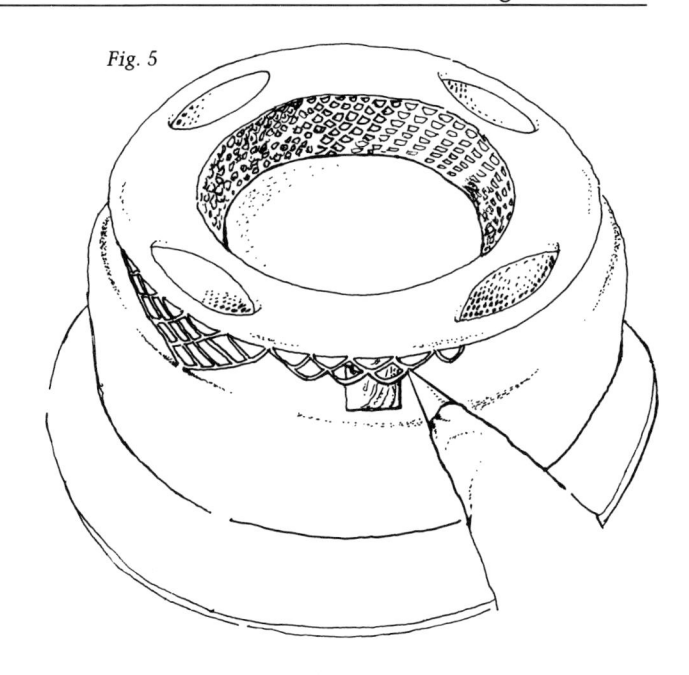

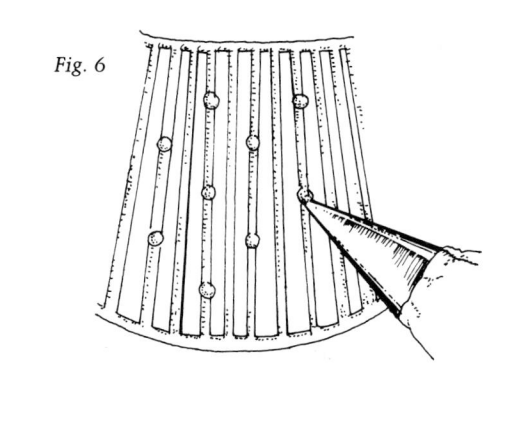

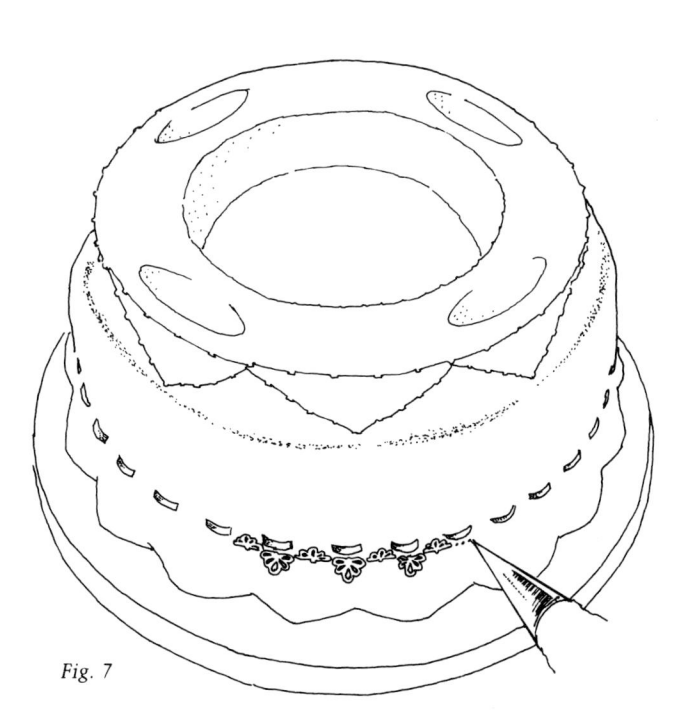

Fig. 7

*Fig. 1*

*Fig. 2*

*Fig. 3*

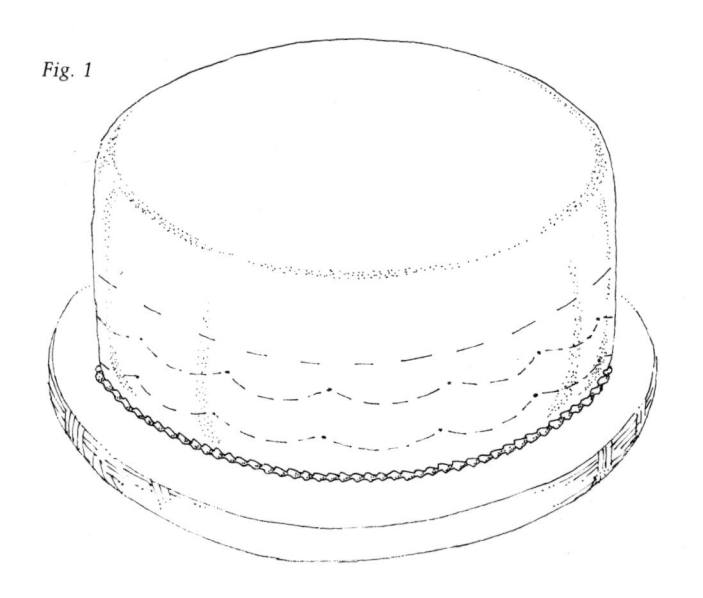

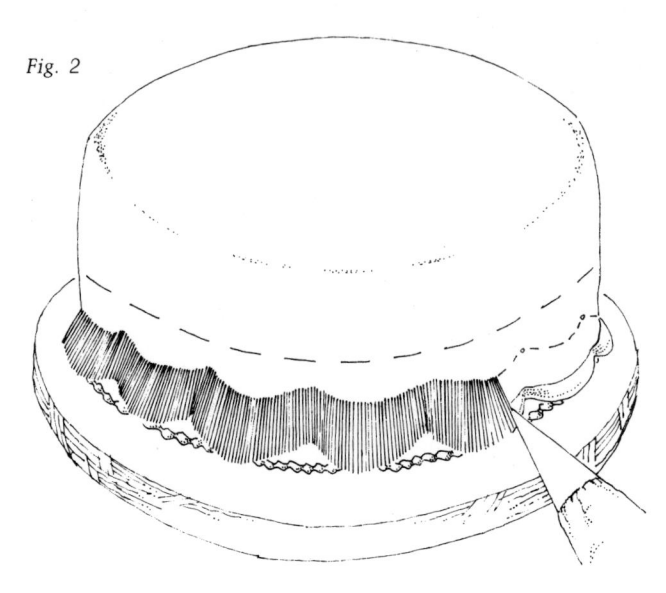

# Green and White Cake

This cake was originally made for display at the 1983 INTERNATIONAL CAKE EXPLORATION SOCIETY. This style combines both layered and upside-down stringwork (oriental stringwork).

The floating collar has since been added, and to keep with the theme of the cake, the upside down stringwork has been piped around the floating collar.

*Step 1:* Make a floating collar (see collars, page 16) and let dry 2 days.
Cover the board with fondant following instructions on page 10, and let dry overnight. Cover the cake with fondant and place on the board. With a #2 tip, pipe a small bead border around the base of the cake and let dry 2 hours.

*Step 2:* Make a false collar and mark the pattern on the sides of the cake (top, middle and lower lines). *See figure 1.* Remove the collar and with a #2 tip, pipe the bridging on the lower marks *only*. Let bridging dry 2 hours then pipe a darker colour of flood icing into the bridging. Let dry overnight. With a 0 tip, pipe the strings from the lower pattern mark to the bridging. Let dry 2 hours. *See figure 2.* With a #2 tip, pipe another set of bridging directly on the top of the pattern mark and the top edge of the strings and let dry. Flood-in with the same shade as the lower bridge, let dry overnight and repeat for the upper set of strings. Let dry. *See figure 3.*

*Step 3:* Around the middle of the cake, pipe upside-down stringwork. Prepare the cake for this design by first dividing the cake around the centre (at the top of the strings) into equal parts. Mark the space with a #1 tip attaching a dot to the strings. Let dry. *See figure 4.*

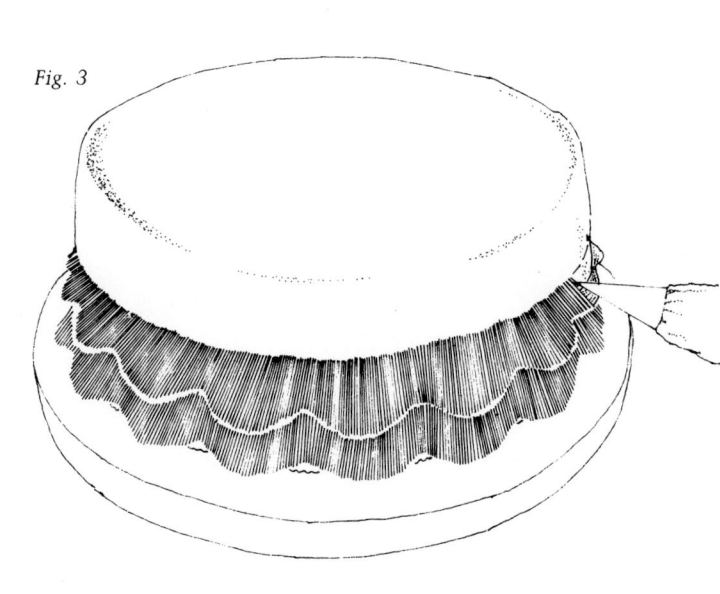

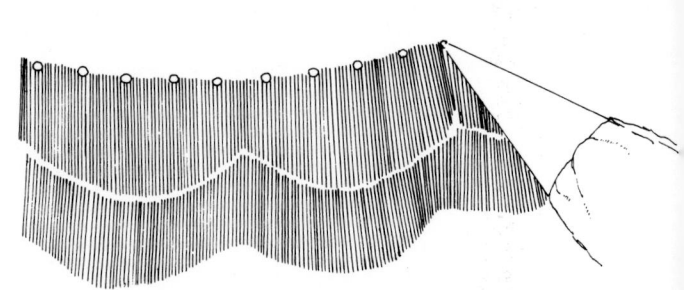

*Fig. 4*

*Step 4:* Make up 2 bags both with a 0 tip, with pale green icing in one bag and white icing in the other. Working with both bags, pipe a scallop from one dot to the third dot in white icing, then with green icing, pipe a scallop from the second dot to the fourth dot. Continue around the cake and let dry 2 hours. *See figure 5.* When dry, very carefully turn the cake upside down and stand the cake on a large (48 oz.) tin or glass jar. *See figure 6.* Repeat the same scallops matching up green to green and white to white. Let dry. *See figure 7.* Repeat the scallops, each time making the scallops gradually smaller (approximately 4 times in all). Let dry. *See figure 8.* Make up lace

*Fig. 5*

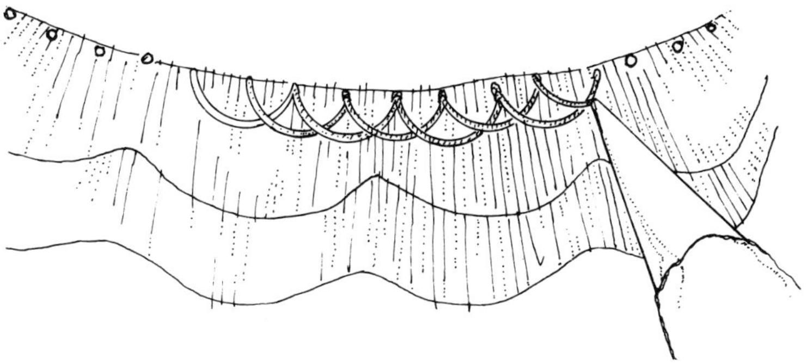

*Fig. 6*

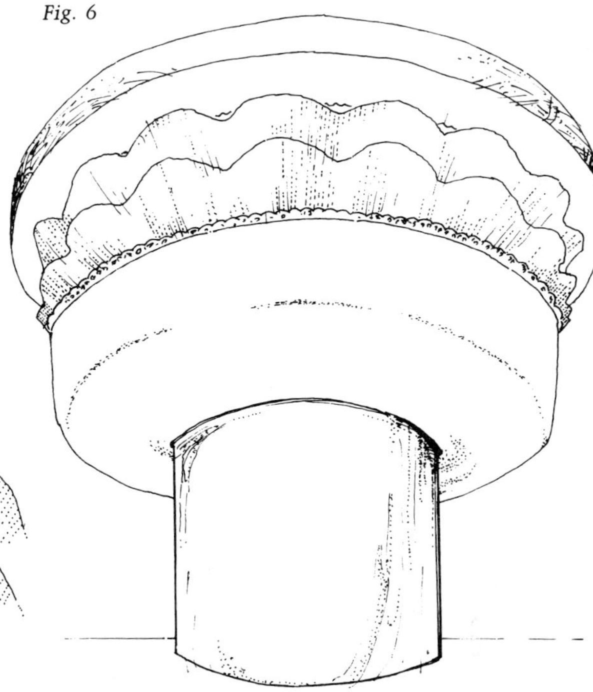

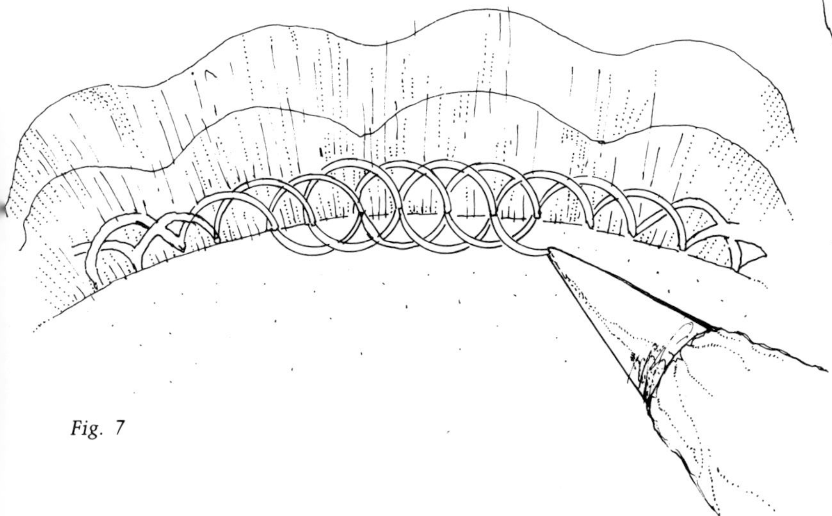

*Fig. 7*

*Fig. 8*

## 82 Floating Collars

*Fig. 9*

*Fig. 10*

*Fig. 11*

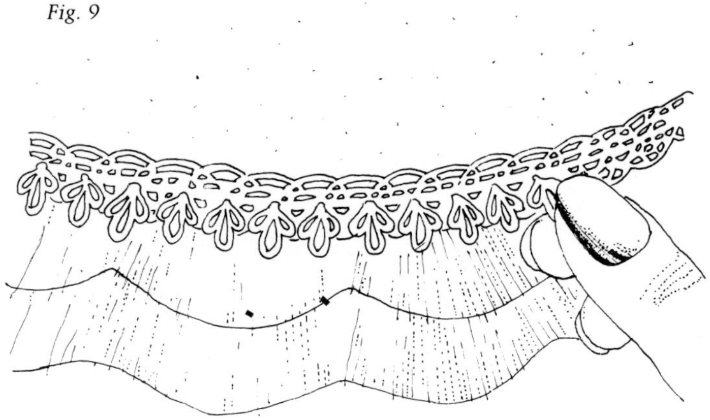

pieces with a 0 tip and let dry. Attach to the centre of the upside-down string work with royal icing. *See figure 9.*

*Step 5:* Mark and pipe the embroidery with a 0 tip and let dry. Pipe the small scallops around the lower edges of both sets of strings and let dry. *See figure 10.*

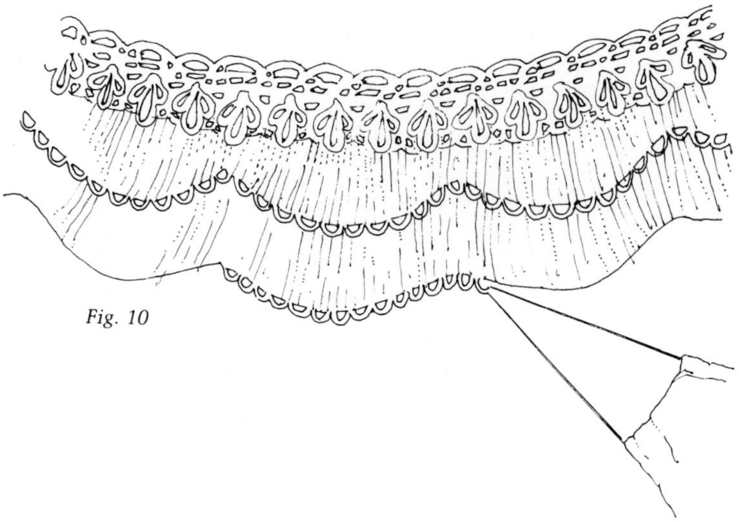

*Step 6:* To attach the floating collar, first place the flood-in collar on top of the cake and mark the outside of the collar on the cake. Remove the collar and pipe a solid line with a #1 tip around the pattern mark. Let dry at least 2 hours.

Centre the wooden blocks on top of the cake. Very carefully place the collar on to the wooden blocks. With a 0 tip, first pipe the inside scallops around the collar, making sure the final scallop touches the cake and let dry. *See figure 11.*

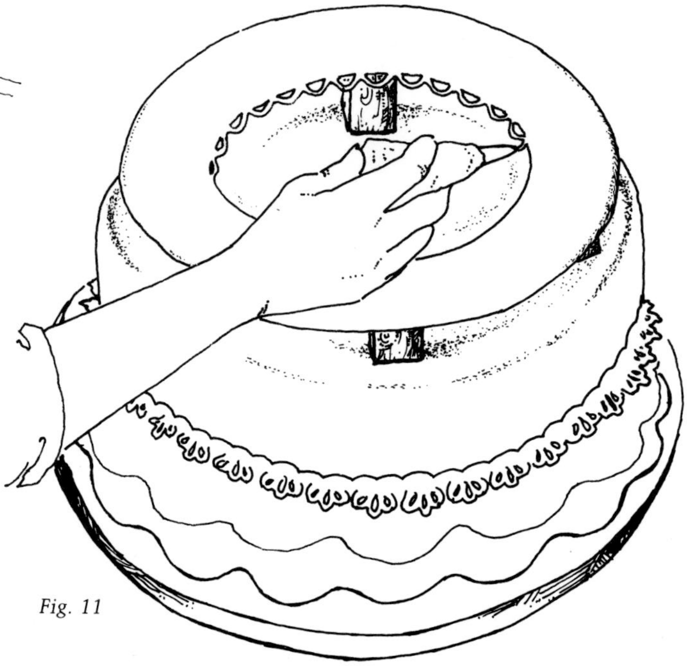

Repeat the outer strings, only this time, pipe strings down from the collar to attach to the bridge line. Work between the blocks and once dry, remove one block at a time and pipe the strings where the blocks have been removed. Let dry. *See figure 12.*

*Step 7:* With a 0 tip, pipe picot around the base of the strings and let dry. Picot is made by first piping 3 dots, then 2 dots above and in between the 3 dots, and finally 1 dot above and in between the 2 dots. *See figure 13.* Let dry. Pipe the upside down string work around the centre of the collar repeating as above. *See figure 14.*

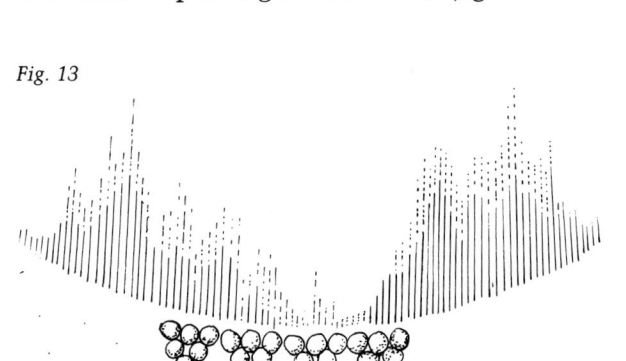

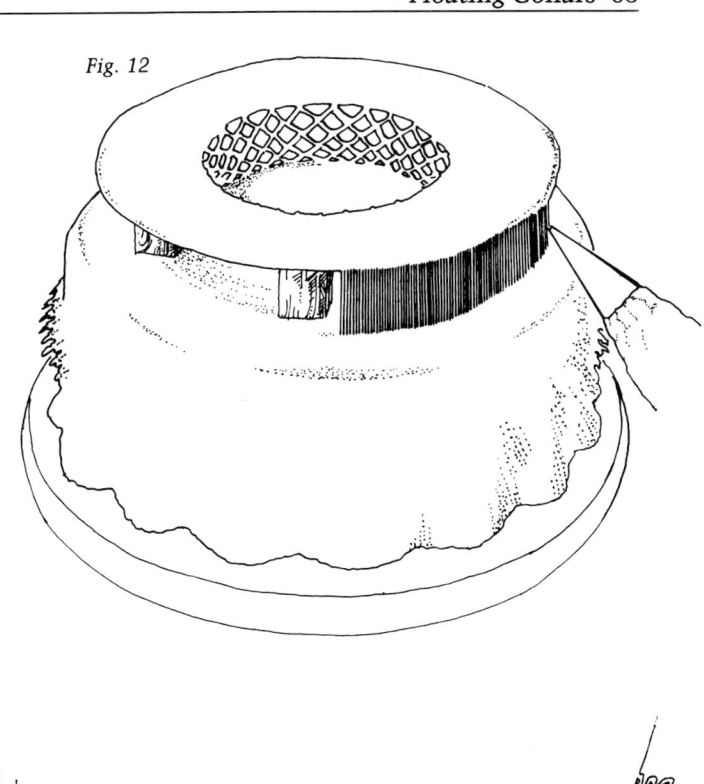

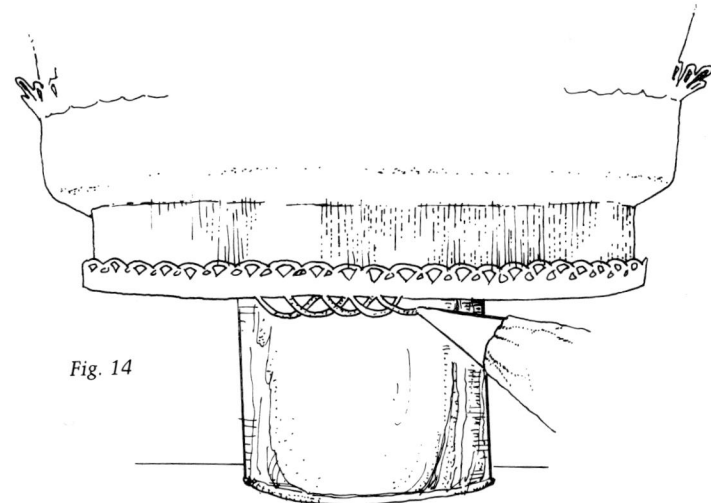

Fig. 12

Fig. 13

Fig. 14

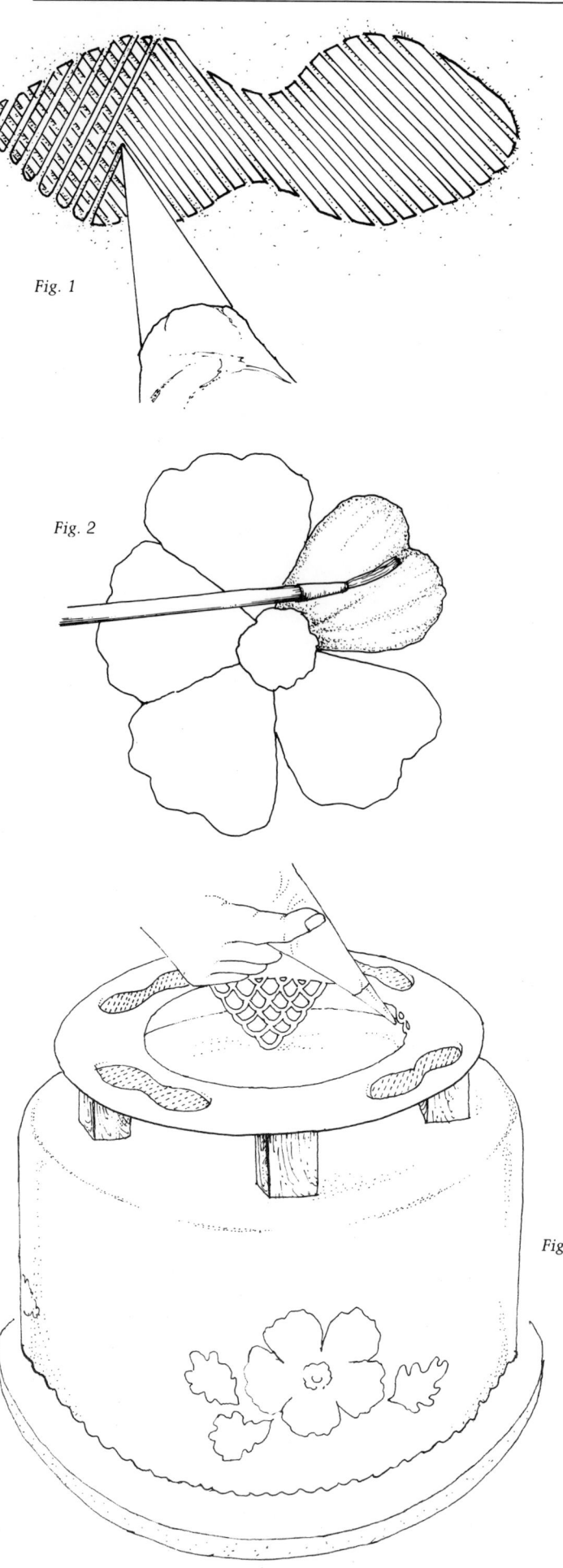

# Two-Tier White Floating Collar Cake

This simple cake combines both brush embroidery and the floating collar.

*Step 1:* Prepare the flood in collars as instructed on page 16. Mark the inner pattern on the collar, and first outline with a #1 tip, then flood-in the collar. Let dry 48 hours. When dry, gently peel the collar off the cooking film, turn the collar over and with a 0 or #1 tip pipe inside the pattern. *See figure 1.*

*Step 2:* Cover both the boards with fondant (following instructions on page 10) and let dry overnight. Cover the cakes with fondant (following instructions on page 11) and attach to the boards.

*Step 3:* While the fondant is still soft take your embossed cards (following instructions on page 15) and press them into the side of the cakes.

*Step 4:* With a #2 tip, pipe a small bead border around the base of the cake. Let dry.

*Step 5:* With a #5 soft brush and a small bowl of water or lemon juice, outline with a #2 tip and royal icing ONLY one petal at a time, and with the damp—NOT WET—brush, brush the icing down from the very top and from the sides in towards the centre and down to the middle of the flower. Repeat until all the pattern has been completed. Let dry. *See figure 2.*

*Step 6:* Place the wooden blocks on top of the cake, and very carefully place the collar on top of the blocks. With a #0 tip first pipe the inside scallop. Let dry. *See figure 3.*

Fig. 1

Fig. 2

Fig. 3

ANNIVERSARY MUSIC BOX

BEIGE CAKE WITH UPSIDE-DOWN STRING WORK

DOUBLE FLOATING COLLAR CAKE

BEIGE DOUBLE COLLAR CAKE, 1983

Floating Collars 89

*Step 7:* With a #0 tip, pipe the outer collar in between the blocks, let dry. Then very carefully remove one block at a time and pipe small scallops. Let dry. *See figure 4.*

*Step 8:* With royal icing to a count of 8, pipe small dots on the joins of the scallops. Let dry. *See figure 5.* Pipe small dots on the inside edge of the floating collar pattern. Let dry. *See figure 6.* Then pipe small dots on both the inner and outer floating collar. Let dry. *See figure 7.* Repeat for the top tier.

*Fig. 4*

*Fig. 5*

*Fig. 6*

*Fig. 7*

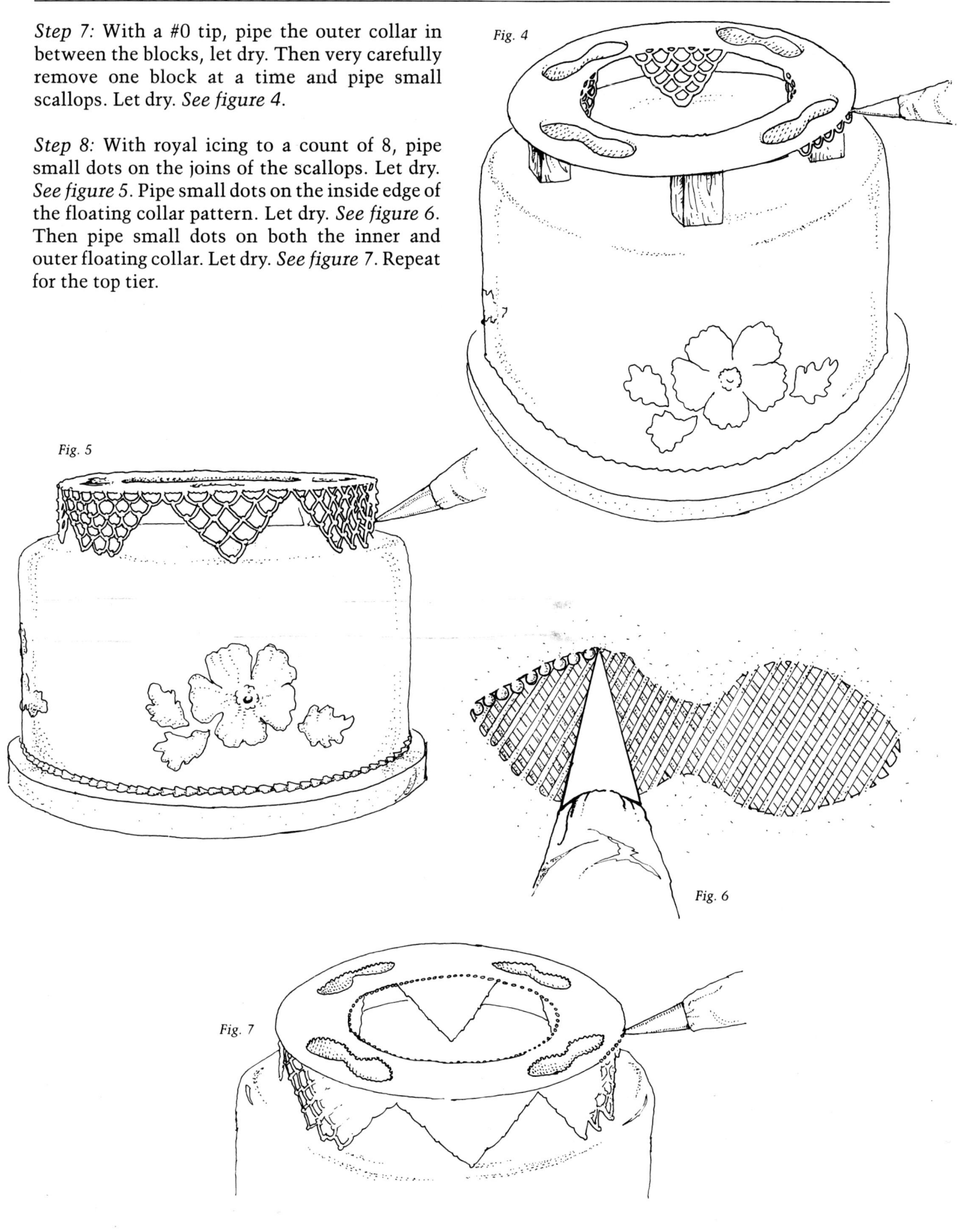

# Two-Tier Pink Cake with Roses

This elegant cake combines both a cut out fondant collar, and a solid flood-in collar.

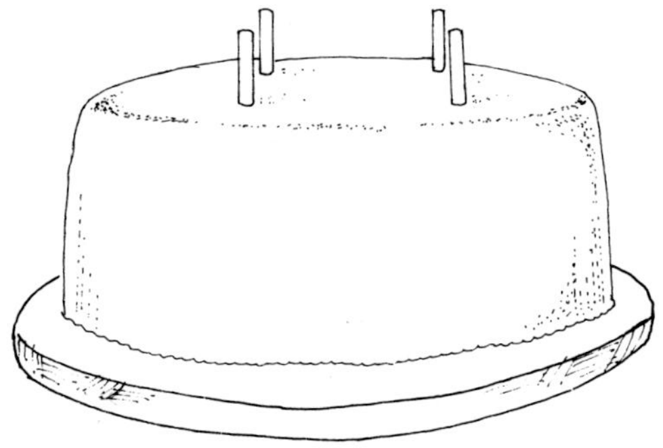

*Step 1:* Cover the board with fondant following instructions on page 10, and let dry overnight. Cover the lower tier with fondant and place on the board. Dowel the lower tier (see dowelling, page 14). *See figure 1.* Cover the top tier with fondant and place the cake on top of the bottom tier. With a #2 tip, pipe a small bead border around the base of both cakes and set aside to dry.

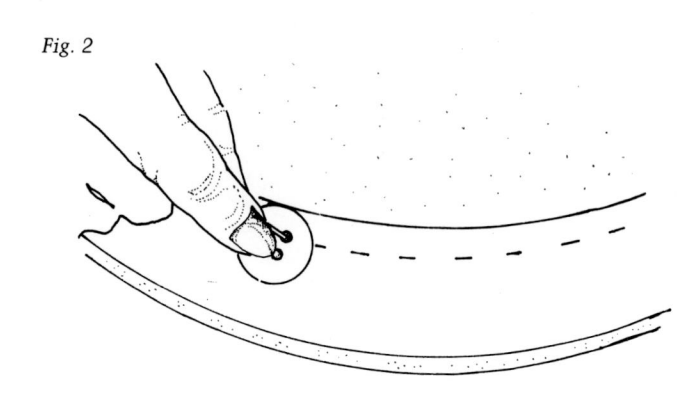

*Step 2:* With a false collar, mark the pattern on the side of the cake with a dressmaker's wheel. With a button and a toothpick inserted through the centre, move the button around the base of the cake, marking a circle on the board. *See figure 2.*

*Step 3:* Using an Xacto knife, cut small slits through the fondant, approximately ½" (13 mm) apart all around the cake to allow for placement of the ribbon. Cut small sections of ribbon (to be inserted into the slits on the cake), making sure they are all the same length, but slightly longer than the width between the slits to allow the ribbon ends to tuck easily into the slits. *See figure 3.*

*Step 4:* Starting on the top tier, and with a 0 tip, pipe the strings down directly on to the top edge of the lower cake and let dry. Repeat for the lower tier, only this time the strings are piped directly on to the bridge line on the board. Let dry.

*Fig. 1*

*Fig. 2*

*Fig. 3*

*Fig. 4*

gum glue

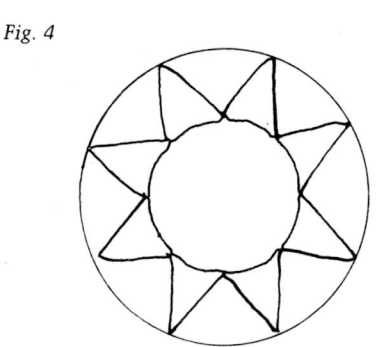

*Step 5:* With run-in royal icing to a count of 8, pipe the small dots on to the strings. Attach the lace pieces, and with a 0 tip, pipe the embroidery around the cakes.

*Step 6:* To attach the floating collar, first make a solid run-in collar and let dry completely. Then make a second collar, only this time make the top collar from fondant the same shade as the cake. Mark the fondant collar like an 8-piece pie, lifting the section up and over. *See figure 4.* (This style of work is called fondant cut outs). Attach the small vase of flowers with royal icing on to the run in collar. *See figure 5.* Attach small bows of ribbon at the eight points of the cut outs. Very gently place the collar on the wooden blocks on the top tier.

*Step 7:* With a 0 tip, pipe the strings between the blocks and let dry. *See figure 6.* Take out one block at a time and pipe in that section with strings making sure that the section dries completely. Repeat until all the blocks have been taken out. As this collar has only the outer strings, you must make sure that the strings are completely dry before you continue.

*Step 8:* Pipe small dots to attach the lace pieces around the edge of the floating collar. Let dry. *See figure 7.*

*Fig. 5*

*Fig. 6*

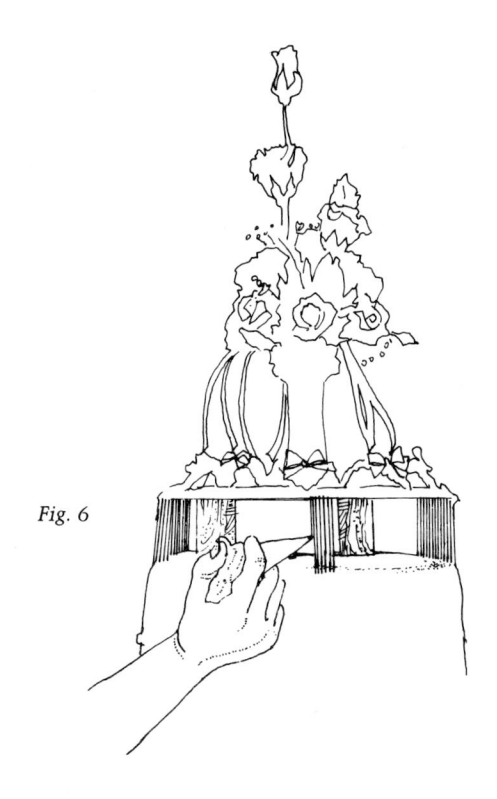

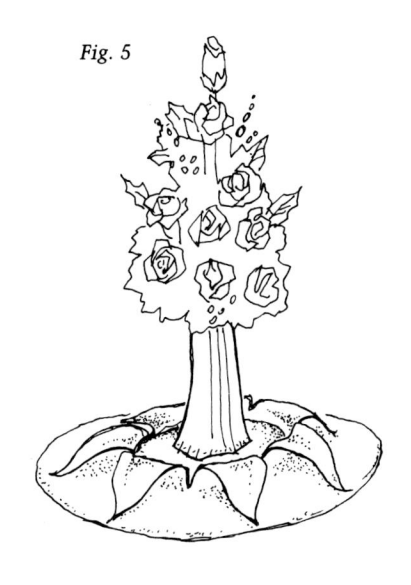

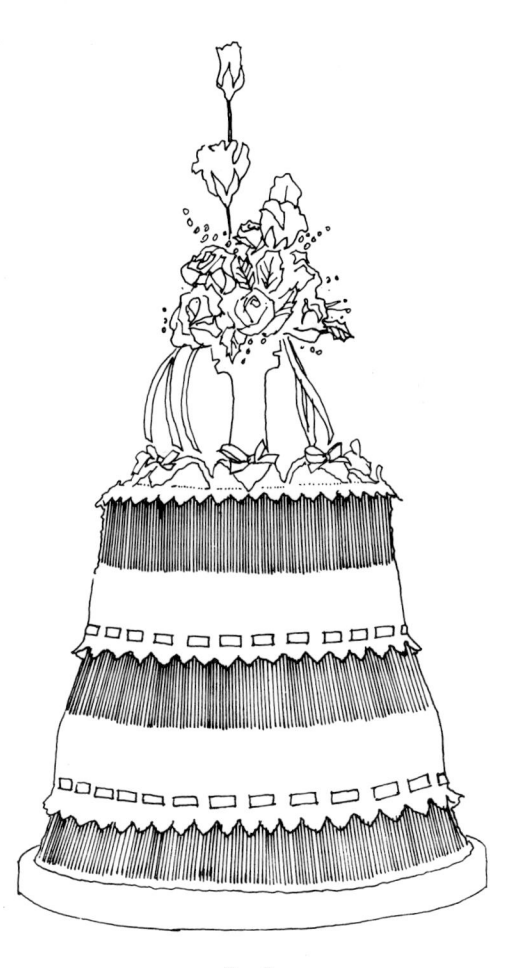

*Fig. 7*

*Fig. 1*

*Fig. 2*

*Fig. 3*

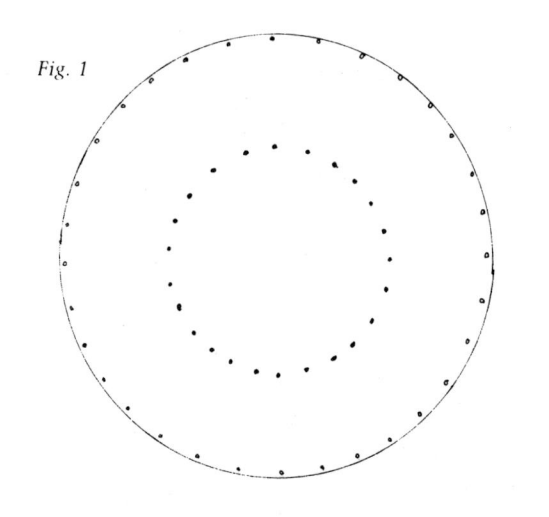

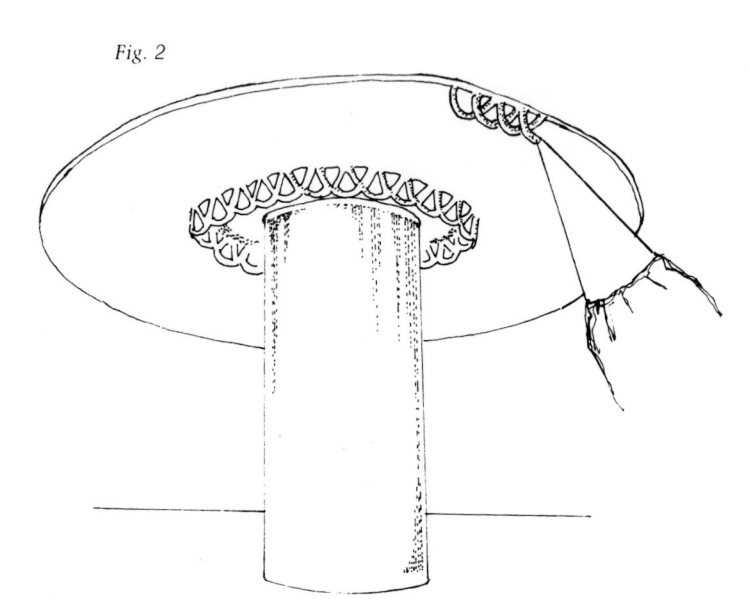

# Beige Cake with Upside-Down Stringwork

This style of floating collar is sitting on the cake which won the "St. Martins" trophy in London, England.

*Step 1:* Prepare and decorate the cake following the instructions on page 78. (See Winning Cake—London).

*Step 2:* Make a solid flood-in collar and let dry (see flood-in, page 16.)

*Step 3:* Place a small glass in the centre of the collar and with small dots, divide the circle evenly for the number of circles required. Repeat for the outer circle and let dry. *See figure 1.*

*Step 4:* Placing the collar upside down on either a straight glass or jar, start with the inner circle and with a 0 or #1 tip, pipe the loops from the 1st dot to the 3rd dot, and from the 2nd dot to the 4th dot. *See figure 2.* Let dry and repeat for the second time, this time making the loops slightly larger. Let dry.

Repeat for the outer collar, but this time, only pipe one line of loops and let dry. Very carefully lift the collar off, taking care not to break any loops, and place the collar on to the blocks on the cake. With a 0 or #1 tip, pipe the loops to match the upside down loop. *See figure 3.* For the second loop, starting in the middle of the lower first loop, repeat until you have reached the top of the cake. Let dry. Very carefully, remove one block at a time, completing the lower loop to form a circle and let dry. *See figure 4.* Again repeat until all the blocks have been removed.

*Step 5:* With royal icing to a count of 8, pipe the small dots both to strengthen and to hide the joints. Let dry. *See figure 5.*

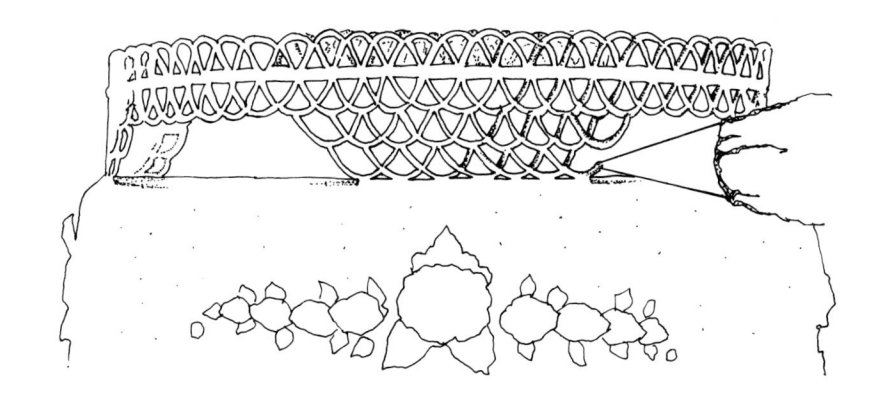

Fig. 4

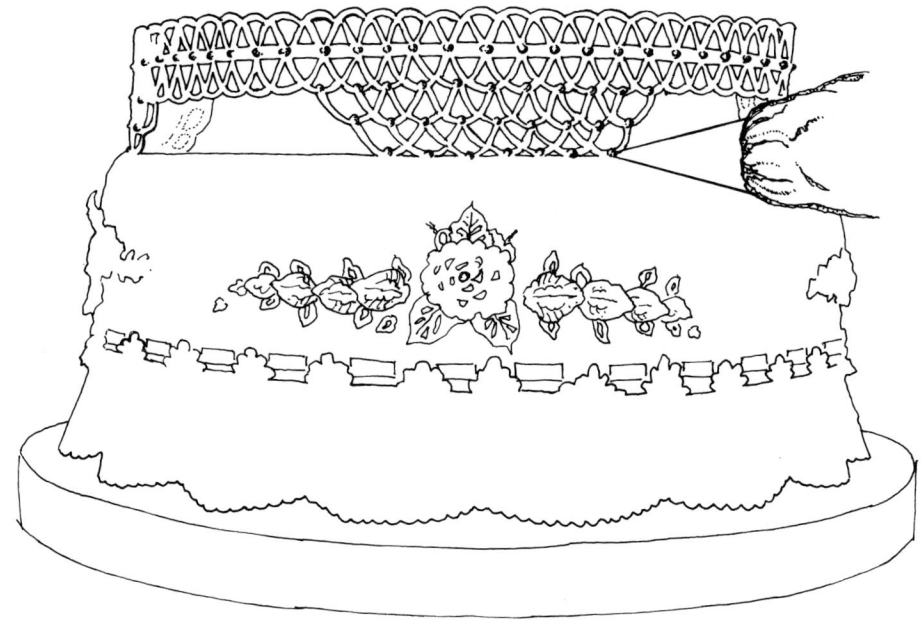

Fig. 5

# Double Floating Collar Cake

This style of floating collar is sitting on the cake which won the "St. Martins" trophy in London, England.

*Step 1:* Prepare and decorate the cake following the instructions on page 78. (See Winning Cake—London).

*Step 2:* First, make the solid flood-in collar by drawing a 7" (17.5 cm) circle. Outline the circle with a #1 tip and royal icing. Following the

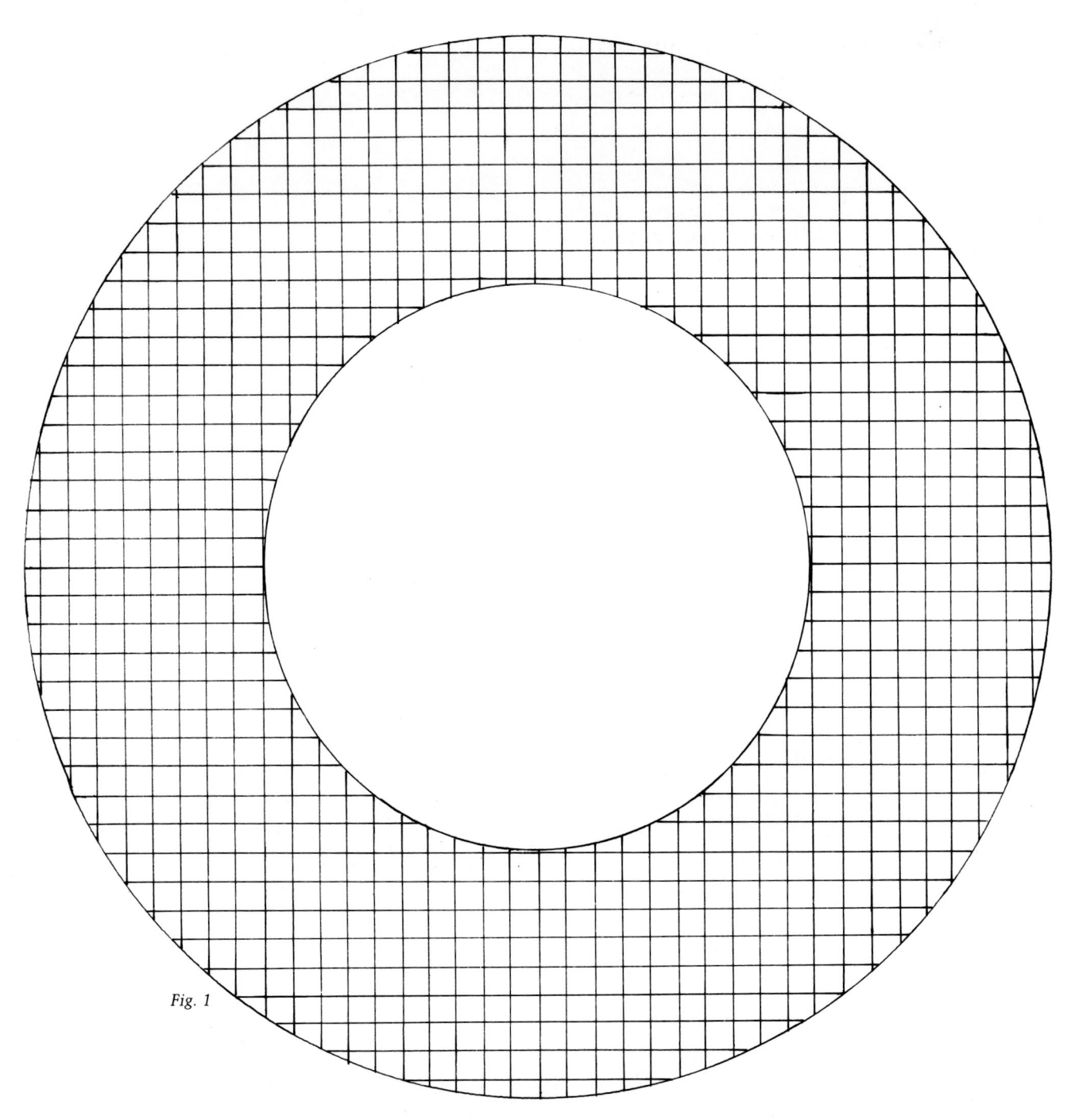

*Fig. 1*

instructions on page 16, make the collar. Let dry 48 HOURS.

*Step 3:* To make the filigree collar, first draw the 7" (17.5 cm) circle. Outline the inner circle only with a #1 tip and royal icing. With a #0 tip, pipe the filigree pattern, then with a #1 tip outline the outer circle. Let dry 24 hours. *See figure 1.*

*Step 4:* Release both collars from the cooking film, and with the solid collar at the bottom, place the wooden blocks on top of the collar. Very carefully place the filigree collar on top of the wooden blocks.

*Step 5:* With a #0 tip, pipe inside the inner circle first with a small scallop. Let dry. *See figure 2.* Then pipe between the wooden blocks on the outer circle. Let dry. *See figure 3.*

*Step 6:* Very carefully remove one block at a time, and at the same time pipe small scallops where the wooden blocks have been removed. Let dry at least 6 hours.

*Step 7:* Place the wooden blocks on top of the cake, and very carefully place the double collar on top of the wooden blocks. With a #0 tip pipe small scallops between the wooden blocks. Let dry. *See figure 4.*

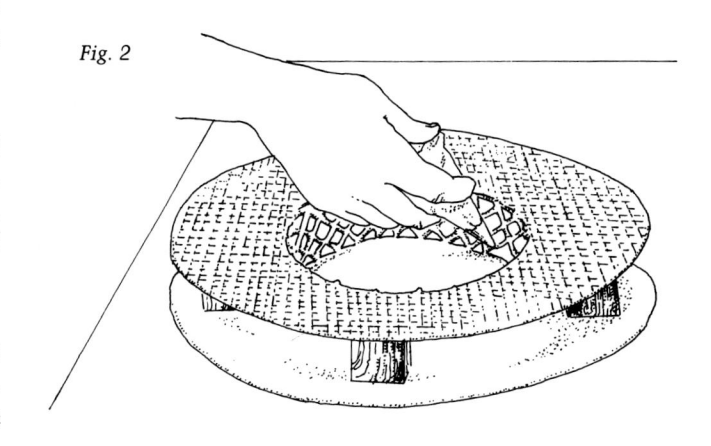

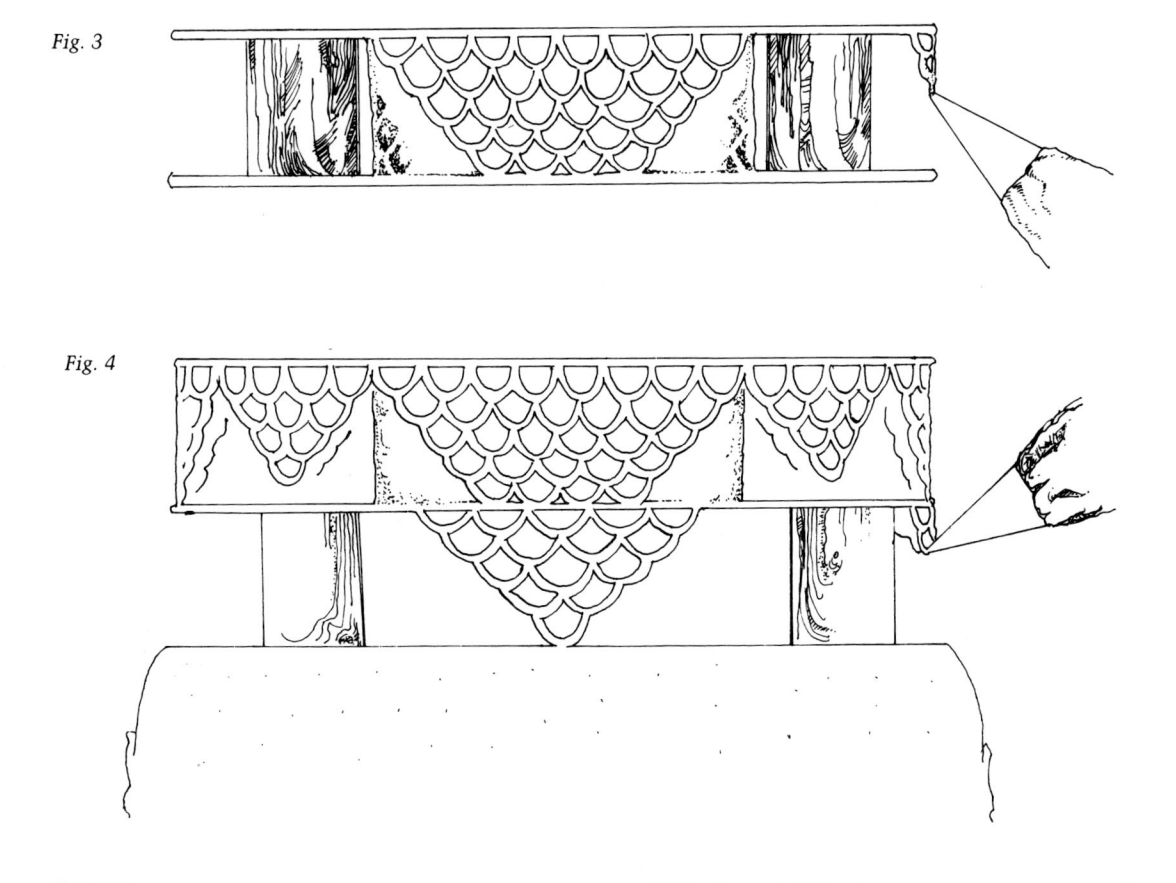

*Fig. 2*

*Fig. 3*

*Fig. 4*

*Step 8:* Repeat as for step 6.

*Step 9:* With a #0 tip, pipe the small embroidery pattern for the top collar. Let dry.

*Step 10:* Pipe a small amount of royal icing on the back of the embroidery pieces, and very gently attach the pieces to the top collar. Let dry. Pipe small dots at the scallop joins. Let dry. *See figure 5 and 6.*

*Step 11:* A small vase of fresh flowers was placed in the centre of the solid collar.
(Note: Please remove the vase before attempting to travel with this style of collar).

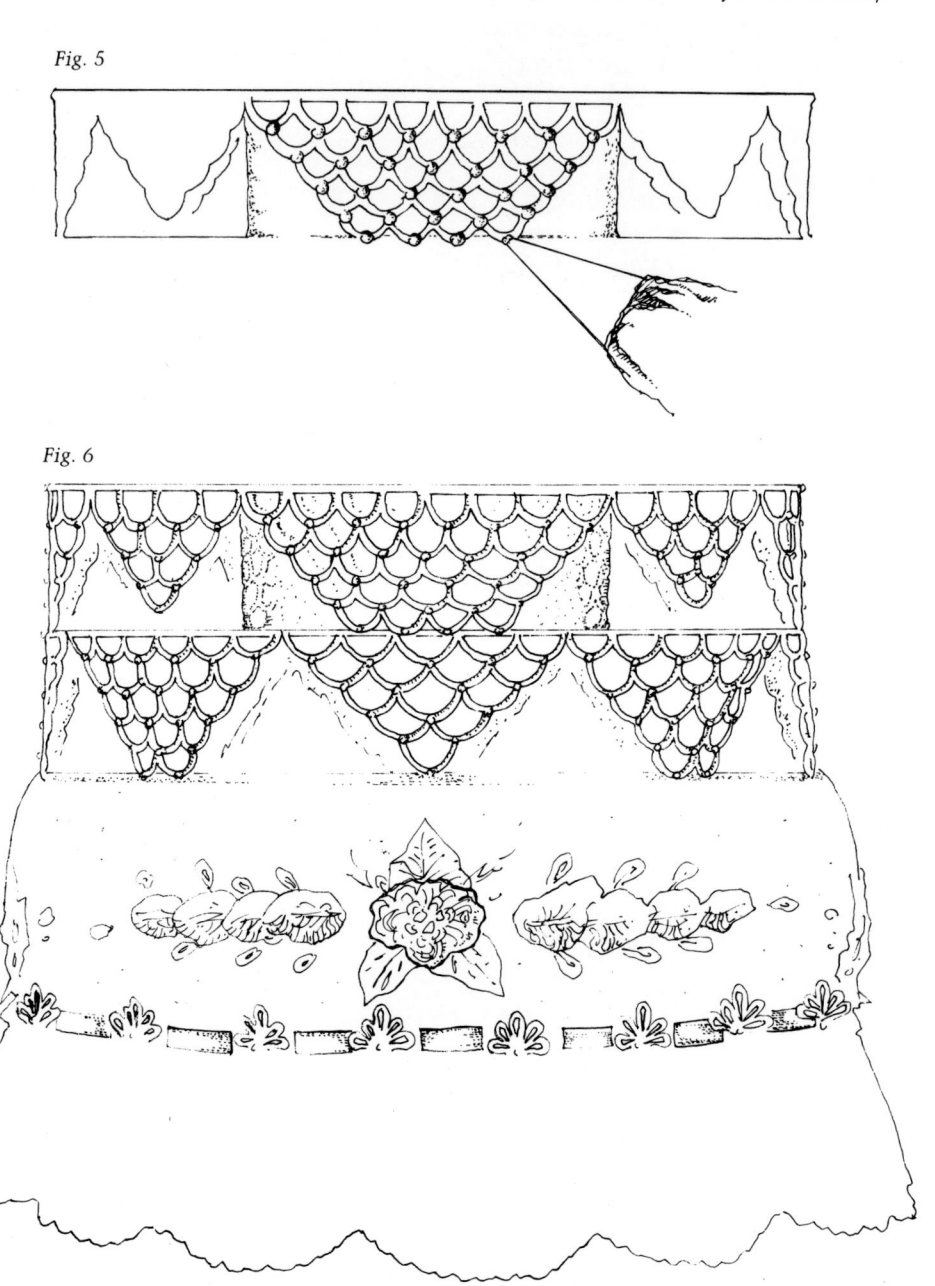

Fig. 5

Fig. 6

# Patterns

TWO-TIER PINK CAKE
AND BLUE ONE-TIER CAKE

GREEN AND WHITE CAKE

BEIGE COLLAR CAKE

BEIGE DOUBLE COLLAR CAKE, 1983

MISCELLANEOUS

MISCELLANEOUS

98 *Embroidery*

BLUE ONE-TIER CAKE

TWO-TIER YELLOW CAKE

TWO-TIER RUFFLE CAKE

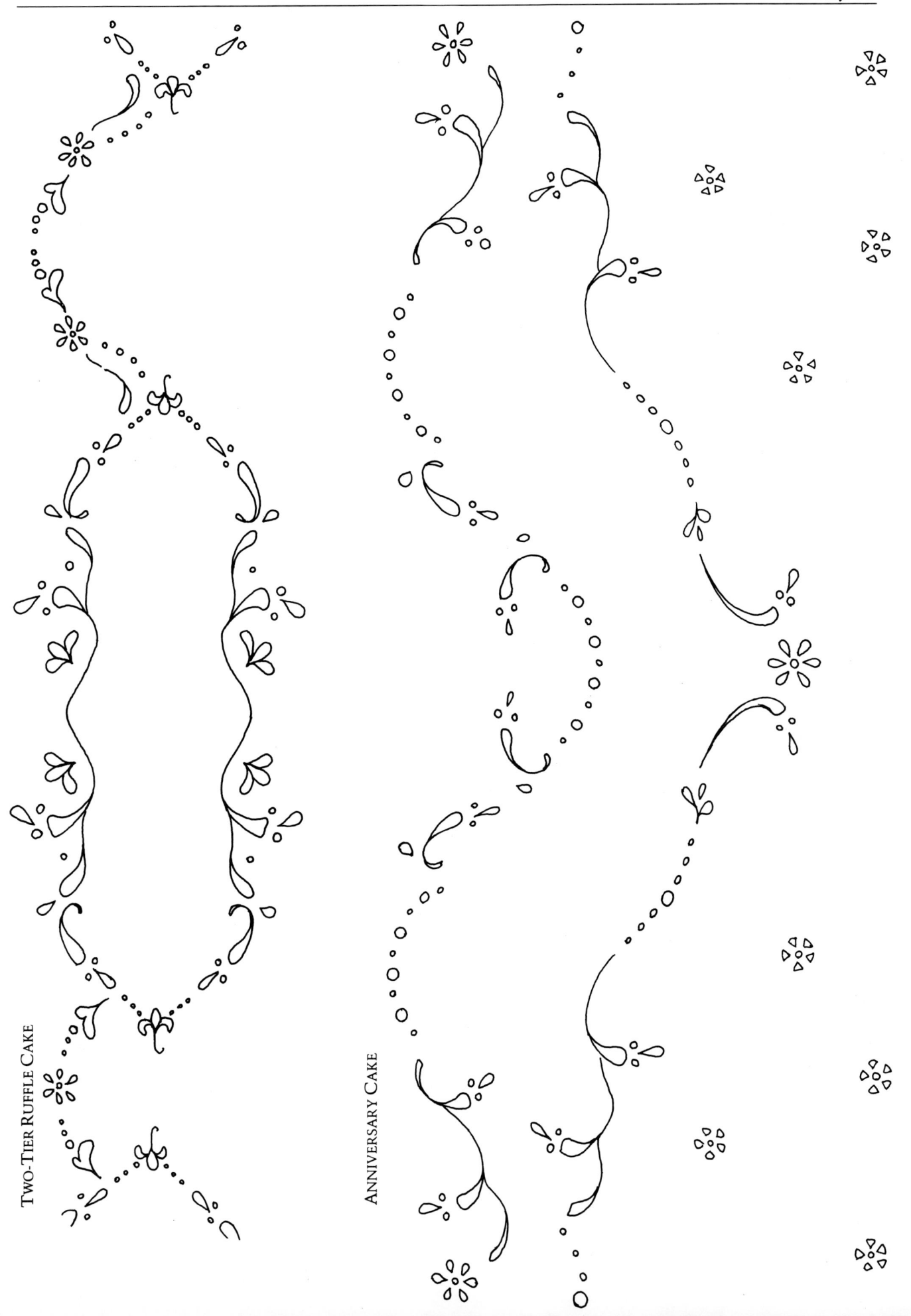

ANNIVERSARY CAKE

100 *Embroidery*

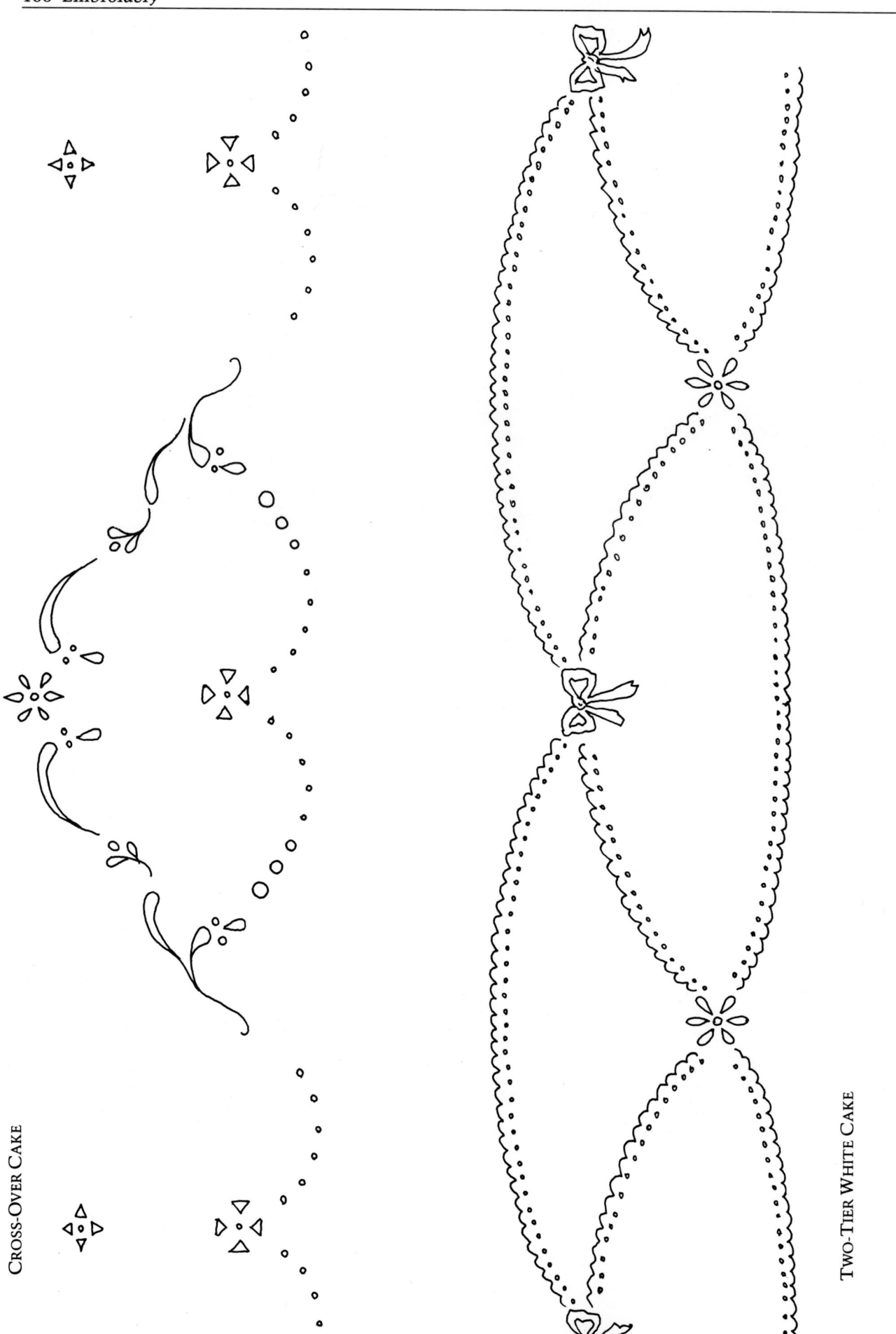

Cross-Over Cake

Two-Tier White Cake

Embroidery 101

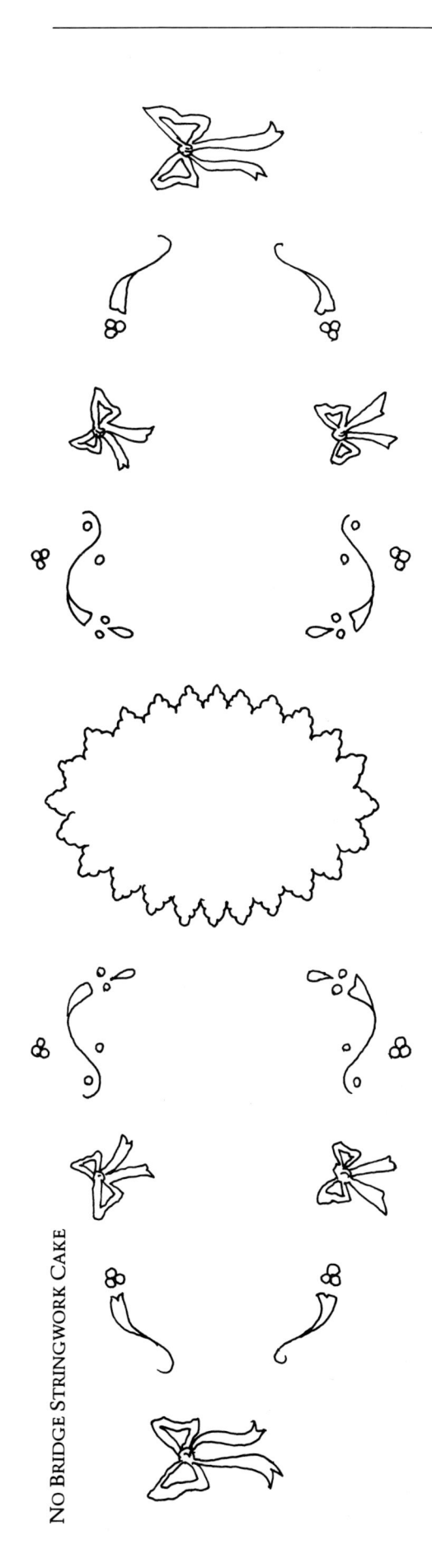

No Bridge Stringwork Cake

Winning Cake From London